A Pilgrimage
of Paradoxes

A Pilgrimage of Paradoxes

A Backpacker's Encounters with God and Nature

Mark Clavier

t&tclark

LONDON • NEW YORK • OXFORD • NEW DELHI • SYDNEY

T&T CLARK
Bloomsbury Publishing Plc
50 Bedford Square, London, WC1B 3DP, UK
1385 Broadway, New York, NY 10018, USA
29 Earlsfort Terrace, Dublin 2, Ireland

BLOOMSBURY, T&T CLARK and the T&T Clark logo are trademarks of Bloomsbury
Publishing Plc

First published in Great Britain 2022

Cover image: Cadair Idris and the Afon Mawddach. 1930s Great Western
Railway poster. Retro AdArchives / Alamy Stock Photo.

Wendell Berry, excerpt from 'What Passes, What Remains' from *The Art of Loading
Brush: New Agrarian Writings*. Copyright © 2017 by Wendell Berry. Reprinted with
the permission of The Permissions Company, LLC on behalf of Counterpoint Press,
counterpointpress.com
W. H. Auden, excerpt from 'Advent' from *For the Time Being: A Christmas Oratorio*.
Copyright © 1944 by WH Auden, renewed. Reprinted by permission of Curtis Brown, Ltd.

A catalogue record for this book is available from the British Library.

Library of Congress Cataloging-in-Publication Data
Names: Clavier, Mark, author.
Title: A pilgrimage of paradoxes: a backpacker's encounters with God
and nature / Mark Clavier.
Description: London; New York: T&T Clark, 2021. | Includes bibliographical references
and index. | Identifiers: LCCN 2021013475 (print) | LCCN 2021013476 (ebook) |
ISBN 9781350252554 (hb) | ISBN 9781350252578 (epub) |
ISBN 9781350252585 (epdf)
Subjects: LCSH: Nature–Religious aspects–Christianity. | Paradox–Religious
aspects–Christianity. | Clavier, Mark–Travel–Wales. | Christian pilgrims and pilgrimages.
Classification: LCC BT695.5 .C545 2021 (print) | LCC BT695.5 (ebook) |
DDC 261.8/8–dc23
LC record available at https://lccn.loc.gov/2021013475
LC ebook record available at https://lccn.loc.gov/2021013476

ISBN: HB: 978-0-5677-0355-2
PB: 978-0-5677-0356-9
ePDF: 978-0-5677-0358-3
ePUB: 978-0-5677-0359-0

Typeset by Deanta Global Publishing Services, Chennai, India
Printed and bound in Great Britain

To find out more about our authors and books visit www.bloomsbury.com and sign up
for our newsletters.

But ask now the beasts, and they shall teach thee; and the fowls of the air, and they shall tell thee:

Or speak to the earth, and it shall teach thee: and the fishes of the sea shall declare unto thee.

Who knoweth not in all these that the hand of the Lord hath wrought this?

In whose hand is the soul of every living thing, and the breath of all mankind.

Job 12.7-10 (AV)

CONTENTS

List of figures ix
Welsh names x
Preface xii
Acknowledgements xvi

1   *Cadair Idris*: Encountering God and nature on a
    Welsh mountain 1

PART I THE PARADOX OF ETERNITY AND
        TIME 15

2   *Cwm Cau*: Timelessness 17

3   *Dysynni Valley*: Thick time 31

4   The Incarnation 46

PART II THE PARADOX OF SILENCE AND
         WORDS 61

5   *Craig Lwyd*: Silence 63

6   *Gwyn ap Nudd*: Words 79

7   Baptism 94

PART III THE PARADOX OF WONDER AND THE COMMONPLACE 111

8 *Penygadair*: The wonderful 113

9 *Rhiw Gwredydd*: The commonplace 129

10 The Eucharist 144

11 Inhabiting *Hiraeth* and *Tangnefedd* 158

Bibliography 173
Index 177

FIGURES

1   Camping in Cwm Cau 15
2   An early morning view down at Llyn Cau 61
3   Looking west towards Penygadair with the Irish Sea in the distance 111

WELSH NAMES

When pronouncing a double l ('Ll' or 'll') in Welsh, you need to place the top of the centre of your tongue on the roof of your mouth and breathe through it. To non-Welsh ears, the sound is similar to 'Kl' but with more air escaping.

Cadair Idris *Ca* as in *cat*; *dair* as in *dire* (though many pronounce it to rhyme with *ladder*). *Id* as in *bid*; *ris* as in *risk*.

Carreg yr Enwau *Ca* as in *carrot*. *Reg* in *regulation*. *Yr* as in ur. *En* as in *encourage*. *Wau* as in *Wyoming*.

Castell-y-Bere *Cas* as in *castle*; *tell* as in *tell* but remember the double 'll' rule. *y* as 'u' in *dungeon*. *Bere* as in *beret* (French flat hat).

Craig Lwyd *Cr* as in *crunch*; *ai* as in *I* (me); *g* as in *great*. *Lw* as in Loo; *yd* as 'id' in *bid*.

Craig yr Aderyn *Cr* as in *crunch*; *ai* as in *I* (me); *g* as in *great*. *yr* as 'ur' in *urban* (but roll the 'r'). *Ad* as in *add*; *er* as in *error*; *yn* as in the word *in*.

Crug Hywel *Cr* as in *crunch*; *ug* as *igloo*. *Hy* as 'hu' in *hundred*; *wel* as in *well*.

Cwm Cau *C* is a hard c as in *coat*; *wm* as 'oom' in *room* but a shorter 'oo'. *Cau* as 'Cai' in *Cairo*.

Dolwyddelan *Dol* as in *doll*; *wydd* as in *with*; *ela* as in elastic then add the *n*.

Dysynni	*Dy* as in *done*; **synn** as in *sun*; *i* as in *India*.
Glyder Fach	*Gly* as in *glug*; *der* as in *Derek*. *Fa* is like the first two letters in *Valentine* ('f' in Welsh sounds like 'v') and then add *ch* which is like the 'ch' in Scottish *loch*.
Gwyn ap Nudd	Gw as in *Google*. *yn* as in *in*. *ap* as in a computer *app*. *Nu* as in *knee*; 'dd' as the 'th' in *the*.
Hiraeth	*Hir* as in *here*; *aeth* as 'ath' in *athlete* but with a longer 'a'.
Llanfihangel-y-pennant	*Llan* as 'lan' in *lantern* (but remember there's a double 'Ll' see above). *y* as 'u' in *dungeon*. *Penn* as in *Pennsylvania*; *ant* as in the insect.
Llyn Bochlwyd	*Llyn* as in *lynx* (but remember about the double 'Ll' see above). *Boch* rhymes with *loch* (Scottish lake); *lw* as in *loo*; *yd* as 'id' in *bid*.
Llyn Cau	*Llyn* as in *lynx* (but remember there's a double 'Ll' see above); *Cau* as 'Cai' in *Cairo*.
Llyn y Gadair	*Llyn* as in *lynx* but remember the double Ll rule (see above). *y* as 'u' in *dungeon*. *Gad* as in *gadfly*; *air* as 'Ire' in *Ireland*.
Penygadair	*Pen* as in *pencil*. *y* as 'u' in *dungeon*; **gad** as in *gadfly*; *air* as 'Ire' in *Ireland*.
Rhiw Gwredydd	*Rhiw* as 'rheu' in *rheumatism*. 'Gwre' as in *great*; *dydd* as in 'dith' in *dither*
Tangnefedd	*Tang* as 'tang' in *tango*; *nef* as 'nev' in *never*; *edd* as 'eath' in leather.
Twyn y Gaer	*Twyn* as you would say 'two in'. *y* as 'u' in *dungeon*. *Gaer* 'Ga' as in *gas*; 'er' as in *error*. *Cau* as 'Cai' in *Cairo*.

PREFACE

I never planned to write a book about climbing a Welsh mountain. I was raised in the American South, though ten years of my childhood in South Florida hardly counts as such. My childhood was no different from that of any other boy growing up in suburban America during the 1980s. I knew of Wales then (I've always had family here), but I visited only a few times in my youth and only ever viewed its craggy mountains from afar. My first clear memory of Welsh mountains is standing outside our rental car by a lake during a family holiday, shivering in the July cold as we ate pasties and tried to admire Snowdon. It wouldn't be the last time I had an experience like that.

I initially moved to *Cymru* to take up a teaching post at St Michael's College in Cardiff.[1] The college was a kind of Hogwarts for men and women training for the ministry in the Church in Wales, the Welsh sister to the Church of England. I had by then been a parish priest for around fifteen years in Maryland and North Carolina, County Durham in the northeast of England and three picturesque villages of north Oxfordshire. Along the way, I had also earned a doctorate and was anticipating a new career in academia. Circumstances would conspire to prevent that from happening, but I didn't know that when I began to write this book. I did sense, however, that my life was about to undergo profound changes, and in that anticipation lay my story's seed.

---

[1]Cymru (pronounced Kum-ree) is the Welsh name for Wales. 'Welsh' and 'Wales' derive from the Old English word for 'stranger'. Welsh is notoriously difficult to pronounce (though actually it isn't so hard once you learn the rules and pick up its cadence). It's an ancient tongue, stretching back to before the Romans came to Britain and enduring a long history that has not generally been kind to its people or their land.

I also came late to walking in mountains. I didn't start in any serious way until I lived outside of Asheville, North Carolina, in my mid-thirties. But once I caught the bug, I took to the wooded slopes of the Appalachians like a mountain goat (though then I was shaped more like an over-indulged bear). While I've never attempted serious alpine climbing, I've spent countless hours following mountain trails, wandering across empty highlands, or in happy reverie atop a breathtaking promontory. I'm never more content than when ascending towards a summit I've never visited; even when the climb aches my muscles, the experience of standing on what seems like the threshold of a wide world thrills me. I can think of no place that contrasts more with the Florida I knew as a child than the cold, often wet, mountains of Wales.

The book itself began as a post for the website *Covenant*,[2] written after I had accepted a job at an Oxford theological college and when I thought I'd be bidding farewell to the Wales that I'd come to love deeply. The reflection bubbled up out of me one morning in the manner of a love letter written before a long, perhaps permanent, departure. As you'll learn if you read this book, that sentiment is an appropriately Welsh place to begin. Though my reflections dwelt on God, nature, society and my own life, it really was and remains an expression of my love for this ancient land. While the darkness of winter and the too-frequent rain can occasionally dampen my Carolina spirits, my heart now belongs very much to her mountains. Cadair Idris and my overnight hike along her slopes crystallized this sentiment for me.

It transpired that my departure from Wales was unexpectedly brief. Less than three years later, I crossed back over the River Severn to take up a new post as Residentiary Canon of Brecon Cathedral, which commands a height that looks towards the Brecon Beacons and across a landscape rich with heritage in mid-Wales. By then my life had changed considerably: my nascent academic career had ended abruptly, and my eighteen-year marriage with a whimper. Though I still had the deep joy of my son alongside me, I had coped with pain, confusion and a feeling of being rudderless until a new life began to present itself. As I crossed back over the Welsh border, I found myself newly married to a Welsh academic (only two days

[2]https://livingchurch.org/covenant/

before leaving Oxford) and looking ahead to a middle-aged life I had never anticipated. That the composition of this book spanned this entire period means that it couldn't but be personal. If my experiences between 2015 and late 2017 changed my life, reflecting on the paradoxes contained in this short book changed my thoughts.

Why any of this would interest others is difficult to answer except by expressing the hope that my pilgrimage of paradoxes will speak to a longing many people know well, be they Christians or otherwise. Though theology plays a prominent role in my story, I think those who don't consider themselves Christian or even religious can appreciate the broad themes I articulate and the stories of my adventures I recount. In both travel and nature writing, there are a great many books that wear Buddhism and Eastern philosophy on their sleeves and at least implicitly reveal the ways these influence how the author relates to nature or the places he or she visits. I'm doing much the same in this book, but with the Christian faith and thought that have shaped not only me but the people who have lived in Wales for nearly two thousand years as well. If my reverie helps you to see Christianity in a different light, so much the better.

This is primarily a book, however, for those who love nature, appreciate history, reflect on God and faith and who may feel a deep dissatisfaction with the world as we have made it. While this is undoubtedly a work of Christian devotion (I am a priest after all), it's equally an expressed yearning for a world both ancient and ever new that's altogether different from the often shallow society in which we now find ourselves. I think a world where we live peaceably amid nature and in the company of our ancestors could be one that's governed less by capricious wills or even our supposed ingenuity than by love and conviviality: a world some have glimpsed perhaps during the early days of the Covid-19 lockdown.

I've encountered that world by lacing up my boots and following the network of footpaths that criss-cross Wales and England, living attentively among the landscapes and heritage of this land. In this sense, my overnight walk on Cadair Idris was no different; yet coming when it did in my life, it somehow brought forcefully to mind the blessing I enjoy in these walks. Not everyone has both the temperament and opportunity to stand among landscapes etched with old memories and feel at home among them.

One final word of explanation. Throughout the book, and especially at the beginning, I use the word 'Catholic'. I know from talks and retreats based on this book that this can cause some confusion. After all, I'm an Anglican, a priest in a church famous for having broken away from the Pope and Catholicism. How can I then say that I'm Catholic? The short answer is that 'Catholic' can be used in two senses. The first and usual way is to refer to Roman Catholics. But 'Catholic' also describes the other end of the spectrum of beliefs and practices from Evangelicals. Broadly, it refers to those kinds of Christianity that emphasize the sacraments (especially the Eucharist or Holy Communion), worship according to set liturgies (like the Book of Common Prayer) and treasure the beauty of ornament, chant and ritual.

But don't worry if you're not a Catholic in either sense of the word (or even a Christian) – if you agreed with everything I have to say, the book wouldn't be worth reading, would it?

ACKNOWLEDGEMENTS

Like any good expedition, this book owes a great deal to people who played a part in helping it reach its goal. Because I have been writing it off and on now for nearly six years, it lies beyond me to thank everyone who has helped, especially those whose conversations have given me new insights or ideas for addressing my subject.

The first person I should acknowledge is Christopher Wells, editor of *The Living Church*. Around twenty years ago, he invited me to contribute to that magazine's website, which eventually provided the opportunity for me to begin connecting my walks and my faith. As I said in my preface, the seed for this book was a post I wrote in 2015, part of which was reprinted in 2020 in *The Living Church* by its editor Mark Michael.

Seeds need good watering and fertilization in order to grow. I was kindly offered opportunities for such intellectual horticulture through invitations to lead retreats and quiet days at Mirfield College, Llangasty Retreat House, St Bene't's Cambridge, and for the agricultural chaplains of Hereford Diocese. I'm grateful to Peter Allan CR, Anna Matthews and Nick Read for their hospitality, and to the participants whose questions and engagement helped me to develop my thinking.

I owe an enormous debt of gratitude to Dewi Roberts for providing me with the pronunciation guide for the Welsh names that appear in this book. Father Dewi stands in a fine tradition of often unsung Welsh clergy, whose love for their homeland is combined with a sense of warm hospitality and outshone only by their priestly devotion. Rhian Parry, of the Welsh Place-Name Society, graciously corrected some of my errors about the Dysynni Valley. Peter Sedgwick, Zachary Guiliano and Will Brown have read parts or all of the manuscript, challenging me where I hadn't thought things through and affirming where they thought me right. Jeff Bilbro was instrumental in helping me towards the book's

ACKNOWLEDGEMENTS xvii

title. Rowan Williams, Frances Ward, and Bill Cavanaugh kindly supported my proposal to Bloomsbury T&T Clark. The help of all these people vastly improved this book.

Finally, I'd like to acknowledge those who have shared walks with me during the past fifteen years. Eric Byrd and Bill Morton joined me regularly during my first proper hikes in the Appalachian Mountains, including an utterly mad one in a blizzard. Jane Carter was a delightful companion on my trek in central Iceland and helped to preserve me through my daring attempt at eating fermented shark. Kildare Bourke-Borrowes showed me fascinating places in north Oxfordshire, fortified me with an excellent conversation, and inspired me with the hope that many years of happy wanders still lie before me. My son, Paul, has joined me many times from his earliest childhood, though the pleasure of walking continues to elude him entirely. My wife, Sarah, has also accompanied me on many adventures, some (like the Tour du Mont Blanc) that required her to overcome a degree of trepidation. Her patience with my obsession with walking falls only a little short of saintly. That we fell in love with each other on walks in the Lake District and in the Cotswolds must be a reason why this pilgrimage of paradoxes is so filled with delight.

Of course, I'd be remiss not to include Cuthbert, my ever-faithful English Springer Spaniel, who has been at my side for most of my hikes since 2011. If I've covered 20,000 miles in that time, the mind boggles to think of the distance his paws have travelled as he has run, bounced and snuffled his way along Britain's footpaths. There's no joy quite like that of a spaniel on a good walk.

Mark Clavier
Brecon Cathedral

1

Cadair Idris

Encountering God and nature on a Welsh mountain

I know many people are Catholic[1] because of the otherworldliness they encounter in ornate liturgies and plainsong chant, the rich array of symbols and the secure embrace of the company of holy saints. They admire richly ordered churches where eyes are irresistibly drawn up towards the ceiling, and hence metaphorically towards heaven. Catholic worship and devotion seem unlike anything ever devised by humankind and, therefore, evoke for them a transcendent God. Stand in Salisbury Cathedral, Notre Dame or the Duomo and try not to think about God. It's impossible. Catholic array and actions communicate the numinous to our senses and this moves many people deeply.

That's not why I'm Catholic. It's the church's earthiness that attracts me – she may look towards heaven, but her feet are planted firmly on the earth. Certainly, her rituals and adornments evoke and express the eternal, that the veil between heaven and earth is thin, even diaphanous. Witness sunlight filter through ancient glass and plumes of incense here in Brecon Cathedral, and you'll easily believe heaven is nearby. But Catholicism wraps her worship in the very tangible, often unremarkable, materials of the earth: bread, wine,

---

[1] I use the terms 'Catholic' and 'Catholicism' in their broad sense as referring to those kinds of Christianity that emphasize the sacraments, especially the Eucharist, and worship according to set liturgies.

water, gold and silver, wood, beeswax, silk, fire, incense, flowers and greenery. These seem to say that the path to God isn't away from the everyday stuff of creation, but through it.

In the northern hemisphere, Catholicism even marks time in conformity with nature's annual diary – Advent heralds the coming of winter and Lent its farewell; Easter celebrates the Resurrection with the early buds of spring; the season of Trinity (or Pentecost) arrays altars, pulpits and priests in green vesture while nature carpets the landscape with leaf and grass. We commemorate the dead on All Saints and All Souls as nature paints the countryside in the rich colours of dying foliage. Traditionally, too, Christians have celebrated the agricultural year by blessing ploughs, praying for fruitfulness, beating the bounds and celebrating the bounty of the harvest. In all of this, the church keeps one eye on the earth even while she adores God. By our worship, we seem to declare that Christians shouldn't worship God unless we're joined by nature.

So, I'm Catholic not because Catholicism gives me a taste of heaven but because she only allows me to do so in the company of the earth. Take, for example, our dependence on the sacraments. If I want to be included among God's family, I must first be bathed in water; if I want to be united with Christ, I must regularly partake of bread and wine; if I want to be filled with the sevenfold gifts of the Holy Spirit, I must have oil smeared on my forehead. It's as though God says that we can't approach him apart from his creation, that he wants nothing to do with us if we come with only our souls and bodies. What else do the sacraments teach us but that we dare not approach heaven by leaving creation behind? Indeed, Catholicism insists that to be with God we must be willing to subject ourselves to the simplest objects of creation: water, grapes, grain and oil. Strange to think that the same ingredients used for baking a pie can also be used for filling the faithful with God's grace. Alongside the wood of the cross, those four ingredients are the earthy elements of our salvation. Without them we're lost.

Part of the wonder of the sacraments is that they also require us to trust creation. The Catholic tradition insists on the absurd idea that we must trust that water, grapes, grain and oil can convey us to heaven. How easy to believe that God wants to save us; how hard for some to accept that he does so by washing us in the ordinary water of baptism. I believe that when I swallow consecrated bread and wine, I receive the Body and Blood of Christ. But that belief rests on my accepting

the strange notion that the One through whom 'all things in heaven
and on earth were created, things visible and invisible' (Col. 1.15) can
be conveyed to me by ordinary baked wheat and fermented grapes.
Can the same oil that I use to cook a meal be saturated with the Holy
Spirit when used to anoint a priest or the sick?

According to the Anglican Book of Common Prayer, we can trust
the simple elements of the sacraments utterly. There, the English
Reformer Thomas Cranmer describes a sacrament as 'an outward
and visible sign of an inward and spiritual grace given unto us,
ordained by Christ himself, as a means whereby we receive the same,
and a pledge to assure us thereof'.[2] The sacramental elements not
only convey 'spiritual grace' but also guarantee visibly that we've
received that grace no matter how distracted or unworthy we may
be. Catholic salvation therefore rests on the conviction that the earth
can be trusted: that water, bread, wine and oil can and do dependably
communicate our God to us. They are, if you will, divine tokens of
love – God's gift of his presence tenderly wrapped in simple objects.

The *Exsultet*, sung in many churches at the Easter Vigil, captures
something of creation's mysterious proximity to God. It is a long,
ancient chant that rejoices in the victory of Easter and involves the
blessing of the Paschal Candle, itself symbolic of the light of Christ.
It's replete with majestic language about Christ's resurrection and
the conquering of darkness by light. Amid this high theology,
however, the cantor sings:

> But now we know the praises of this pillar,
> which glowing fire ignites for God's honour,
> a fire into many flames divided,
> yet never dimmed by sharing of its light,
> for it is fed by melting wax,
> drawn out by mother bees
> to build a torch so precious.[3]

[2]*Book of Common Prayer and Administration of the Sacraments and Other Rites
and Ceremonies of the Church According to the Use of the Church of England*
(Oxford: Oxford University Press, 1925), 299.
[3]Catholic Church, *Roman Missal*, 3rd edn (Chicago: Liturgical Training Publications,
2011), 356.

The image of mother bees building the precious Paschal Candle with their wax immediately grounds the exalted language about God and redemption in the everyday activity of insects. That's what I love about Catholicism – we can't even celebrate Easter without including the bees.

I know many find this sort of thing too mystical, even a little superstitious. And I can see why: the belief that actual water washes away immaterial sins or that wheat and fermented grapes can be drenched through with Christ *is* absurd! On the other hand, I've never really understood why this is any stranger than believing that God can fill human beings with his Spirit. If I can be a vehicle of God's grace, why not bread and wine? Paul preached to the Athenians that God is he in whom we 'live and move and have our being' (Acts 17.28) and wrote to the Romans that 'from him and through him and to him are all things' (Rom. 11.36). God who's beyond everything is also within everything. What's then to prevent him from being within water, grapes, grain and oil to our spiritual benefit? The acacia wood of the Ark of the Covenant contained God's presence as did the richly adorned walls of the Holy of Holies in the Temple in Jerusalem. Eden was so vibrant with the glory of God that he seemed to stroll there in the cool of the evening. How else did Balaam's ass scold his master except by receiving the power of God to do so? No, it seems to me that restricting God's grace to human beings requires one to accept the notion that we somehow stand apart from creation – worse, it suggests that God himself isn't free to do with his own creation as he pleases. Who are we to say what he can't do with the simplest elements of the earth?

So, the commitment to hold both heaven and earth together is why I'm Catholic. If you want to find an otherworldly religion, turn to those forms of Christianity that insist that the Christian armed only with a Bible can approach God without sparing a thought for creation. Megachurches awash with artificial light and amplified sounds created by miked-up preachers, electrified musical instruments and multimedia presentations are to me places far more detached from the world than any monastery. How can we be mindful of the earth in these artificial environments? Indeed, how much harm is done to creation just to provide their hi-tech worship? Where is there room for the humble bee in such places? For me, these churches are the logical consequence of a Christianity that discards the sacraments – reject them and you run the danger of also rejecting the earth as we see in many conservative versions of Evangelicalism in America. And that's why I'm a Catholic.

-o0o-

I probably never would've discovered the reason for my Catholicism were I not also deeply in love with nature. I spend a great deal of my free time outdoors. I regularly go for short walks through fields and along riverbanks and longer ones in mountains and along coastal paths. I've backpacked in the Appalachians, the Brecon Beacons and Snowdonia in Wales, the Sunnmøre Alps in Norway, among the hot springs and glaciers of Iceland, the high passes of the Alps, from Grenoble to Avignon among vineyards and fields of lavender and along the dry, rocky paths of the high Pyrenees with their crystalline lakes. I'm out in all conditions with my wife Sarah and our two spaniels Cuthbert and Humphrey exploring new landscapes or becoming deeply conversant with familiar ones. As a result, during the past eight years, I've rambled more than 20,000 miles, equal to 80 per cent of the earth's circumference.

There are two kinds of walks: those in the company of others and those that are solitary. The former affords time for long conversations with friends and companions – the countryside seems to lend itself to deep discussions. There's something about being out in nature that drops our social defences and draws out our intimate thoughts and feelings. One of the most famous examples of this are the walks that J. R. R. Tolkien and C. S. Lewis took along Addison's Walk by the Cherwell in Oxford – those strolls not only cemented their fateful friendship but also drew from Lewis the kind of questions that led him to become a Christian. If only we had an account of the conversations Paul and Luke must have shared while on their missionary journeys or that St Francis and his companions enjoyed during their holy wanderings. At least we're told about a memorable walk along a road to Emmaus that ended with a meal that opened eyes and inflamed hearts.

The other kind of walk is the solitary one when we can be absorbed into the landscape. While I treasure days out with friends and especially my wife, I find nothing else quite like losing myself in the beauty and wonder that nature conjures. I'm immersed in the surrounding splendour, noticing tiny details like wildflowers, the shape of a leaf, the song of thrush and nuthatch or the way light filters through the canopy of a forest. Starved of conversation, my senses extend to fill the void and by doing so bring the scenery around me closer. I feel younger through the experience, too, as though the boy who delighted in his natural surroundings is lurking just behind the next tree, ready to greet me. This is, I suppose, what's now called mindfulness, but it might be better described as sensuality, for the mind is enlivened through the awakening of the five senses. It's then that I start to *perceive*, experiencing everything around me in a more complete way rather than through just my eyes and at a distance.

When I walk alone, I also start to become acquainted with the *sense* of places that comes only by closely observing how natural features relate to each other within a landscape: the way a solitary oak tree stands in a meadow or a craggy knoll divides a river from the steep slopes of a mountain. This requires an artist's eye, observing in a way that takes in the particulars without losing sight of the whole, as though my mind were saying, 'an outcropping of rock is just the thing for that steep slope' or 'this rich, green grass is perfect for these bleach-bark birches'. Only, the work of the Artist has already been completed; we simply observe and enjoy. Such sensory companionship with nature is the main reason why I walk – I'm drawn out my front door by the deep contentment that comes from regularly rejoining the company of the good earth rather than for the health benefits gained. I don't understand how people stay sane without doing the same.

You don't really begin to know the sense of a place until you've experienced it through a full cycle of seasons and, even then, only when you do so consciously. Such knowledge bears some resemblance to human friendship: the way you know someone only after you've shared their company through the highs and lows and different seasons of their life. Perhaps there's also something about being present in familiar places during the variable seasons of your own life. Often when I walk in deeply familiar places, thoughts and moods from previous walks suddenly pounce on me as though they continued to haunt the paths after my earlier visits.

On most early mornings I take the dogs for a two-mile walk through the ancient woodland that stretches northward from the walled, medieval close of Brecon Cathedral where I now live in Wales. Morning walks first became a habit when I lived in a small village in rural Oxfordshire. My route would take me by the primary school, up a path through a small wood populated by stout beeches and mighty oaks, and then down an old farm track that has demarcated the wood from farmers' fields since the Middle Ages. Later when I first moved to Wales, I strolled in the early hours along a disused railway track with boggy fields on the one side and views of high hills on the other. And when I became principal of St Michael's College, my morning walks took me past the medieval Llandaff Cathedral and along the Taff, often in full flood from the frequent Welsh rains. For just over a year, my wife Sarah (whom I was then dating) and I would meet each morning to walk through Aston's Eyot in Cowley outside Oxford or along the Thames and down the ancient streets as that old city awoke.

In each place, encountering a landscape with its sights, smells and sounds at the same time of day in every season has produced a feeling of cosy familiarity – indeed, I experience each season like the ebb and flow of the tide. The first hints of spring swell into the full blush of May and early June before peaking with the seasoned lushness of high summer. I see and feel the approach of winter in mid-autumn, experience it getting colder, muddier and darker until the frosts of January and February, and enjoy its often reluctant retreat before the advance of a new spring. You come to know the earth profoundly when you share the seasons with it daily.

For me, a deep familiarity with the landscape also has something to do with light. My morning walks mean that in the course of the year I'm out in complete darkness, soft sunshine and everything in between. The transition from winter's darkness into the clean light of spring and then gradually back towards mid-autumn gloom marks my year even more than the calendar. Landscapes are marvellously transformed by seasonal sunlight here in Britain so that well-known places can suddenly seem new and unfamiliar in late autumn or early spring. The angle of northern sunrays subtly alters colours, creates long shadows where you're not used to them and highlights features that have previously passed you by.

I once enjoyed a memorable evening climbing Fan Fawr in the Brecon Beacons bathed in otherworldly light as the setting sun and thinning mist fused to paint the sky, air and landscape a rich gold. Even my dog Cuthbert seemed mesmerized – one of my favourite photos is of him near the summit of Fan Fawr gazing pensively across the steeply descending slopes towards the setting sun. If you've seen with your own eyes how light can transform an ordinary landscape into a place fit for the gods, you'll probably have less trouble believing that everyday elements can be transformed into sacraments fit for God.

That I observe nature in my worship and God during my walks in the countryside probably reveals more about me than I care to admit. Aren't my experiences the opposite of how it should be? Doesn't God spend his time lurking in churches while Mother Nature goes about her business outside? Should I not focus on heaven in my worship and just enjoy the countryside when I'm outdoors without any fanciful thoughts about God? On the other hand, many people might say that, no, I'm exactly right: God isn't found in buildings or in any organized religion – religion is nothing more than human artifice, a way of controlling people and their longings for the divine. If you want to be spiritual, go for a walk in the woods or play golf.

But please don't misunderstand me: I'm not saying that I meet God in one place and creation in the other; rather, it's the *paradox* that catches my attention. In outward appearance, Catholic worship *seems* to proclaim God in his heaven: what's most apparent in the readings and rituals is the transcendent Deity we worship. Likewise, the most obvious thing about the beautiful countryside is how it proclaims nature's abundance. Both statements are true enough. But because they are true, I'm powerfully struck when I find water, bread, grapes, oil and beeswax in worship and when the sublime delights experienced during my treks draw my attention irresistibly to God. In one place, I'm reminded that God still fills even the humblest objects with his glory (as with the Ark of the Covenant) and in the other that creation by its beauty reaches up to God – both testify to the truth that (in the oft-quoted words of Gerard Manley Hopkins) 'The world is charged with the grandeur of God'.

My attention isn't drawn, however, by the incongruity of earthly elements joining in heavenly worship or of a divine presence felt during country rambles. I have no sense that God or creation are imposters creeping in where they don't belong. It's the opposite – what draws my attention is the profound fittingness or appropriateness of it all, that God and creation somehow belong so obviously together that it's hard to imagine anyone thinking otherwise. It's like when two people with little in common come together in love or friendship and then seem always to have been meant for each other.

This is in part what Roman Catholics, Anglicans and Lutherans celebrate when they recite the *Benedicite:*

Bless the Lord sun and moon:
    bless the Lord you stars of heaven;
    bless the Lord all rain and dew:
    sing his praise and exalt him for ever.
Bless the Lord all winds that blow:
    bless the Lord you fire and heat;
    bless the Lord scorching wind and bitter cold:
    sing his praise and exalt him for ever.
Bless the Lord dews and falling snows:
    bless the Lord you nights and days;
    bless the Lord light and darkness:
    sing his praise and exalt him for ever.
Bless the Lord frost and cold:
    bless the Lord you ice and snow;
    bless the Lord lightnings and clouds:
    sing his praise and exalt him for ever.
O let the earth bless the Lord:
    bless the Lord you mountains and hills;
    bless the Lord all that grows in the ground:
    sing his praise and exalt him for ever.
Bless the Lord you springs:
    bless the Lord you seas and rivers;
    bless the Lord you whales and all that swim in the waters:
    sing his praise and exalt him for ever.
Bless the Lord all birds of the air:
    bless the Lord you beasts and cattle;
    bless the Lord all people on earth:
    sing his praise and exalt him for ever.
O people of God bless the Lord:
    bless the Lord you priests of the Lord;
    bless the Lord you servants of the Lord:
    sing his praise and exalt him for ever.[4]

---

[4]Church of England, *Common Worship: Services and Prayers for the Church of England* (London: Church House, 2000), 778.

When we lose sight of how worship and creation fit each other, we divorce God from his creation and focus his attention too narrowly on us humans. That's just a short step from believing that nature exists primarily to be exploited for our own benefit. I think we need the sacramental paradox of a transcendent God who fills all creation in order to understand either God or nature properly – in fact, I think without that paradox we forget who we are as well.

And that thought takes me to the final realization that has come from my Catholic faith and my long treks in the countryside: how out of place our own modern world is in this setting. God and creation may be perfectly suited for each other, but our own society seeks to suit itself to neither. We have purged God and nature from our habitations, embracing, instead, a way of life that seeks to stand apart from both through a colossal act of collective will. The longer I have been an Anglican and an outdoorsman, the more I've become convinced of our social and cultural exile from our sources of meaning and purpose. And yet, both God and nature continue to haunt us, calling us to return to their glad company, to find our joy and contentment in our companionship with them both.

-oOo-

All of this first came strongly to my mind during a weekend spent backpacking on Cadair Idris in west Wales. For those unfamiliar with Cadair Idris, it's the southernmost mountain of any stature in Snowdonia National Park, which covers much of northwest Wales. To the south is the seaside town of Aberystwyth, home to the National Library of Wales, a decent university and (I must add) a good tobacconist. The Irish Sea lies along its western slopes – today its beaches are cluttered with holiday parks and small communities that attract tourists during the summer. With an elevation of 2,930 feet, Cadair isn't a high mountain by global standards. But its pinnacle, Penygadair, soars above the sandy shoreline of the Irish Sea, making the mountain seem more monumental than its taller companions in the national park. Except for a few old woods and areas of recently planted tree plantations, Cadair Idris is largely barren: its primary features are thick peaty turf, crags and scree. No human habitation is to be found above 1,300 feet, except for a low, concrete bothy erected among the rocks near the pinnacle where backpackers may spend the night.

It was during two days of hiking in Cadair Idris in the autumn of 2015 that I encountered God in a way that made me keenly aware of certain paradoxes. There's a long tradition of finding God up in the mountains. Moses found him in a burning bush on Mount Horeb and in his glory on Mount Sinai (though they're probably the same place). Elijah lived in his cave with God on Mount Carmel and there drew on YHWH's power to outclass the priests of Baal. The holy Temple was built on Mount Zion, and Peter and John witnessed a transfigured Jesus on Mount Tabor. St Anthony wrestled with demons and inspired the first monks on a mountain near the Red Sea in Egypt. St Benedict dwelt as a hermit with God in the Simbruini Mountains before later founding his famous monastery atop Monte Cassino. And it was by climbing a metaphorical Mount Carmel that St John of the Cross found that 'high state of perfection' that is the 'union of the soul with God'.[5] Indeed, he even made his contemplative climb while shut in a gloomy cell, declaring:

> Seeking my Love
> I will head for the mountains and for watersheds;
> I will not gather flowers,
> Nor fear wild beasts;
> And will go beyond strong men and frontiers.[6]

God, it seems, enjoys lurking on mountaintops, which will come as no surprise to those who have stood upon them.

Unlike the patriarchs, disciples and saints, I can't claim to have experienced a mountaintop theophany during my trip up Cadair Idris. As ever in my life, I encountered God more in hindsight – I'm much better at discerning where God has led or has spoken than where he might be leading or what he might be saying. He usually seems to have just exited the room by the time I think to look for him, leaving only the faintest trace as a clue to where he might be going and how I should follow. His presence is like a lingering perfume that can't be missed, though it can be savoured

---

[5] John of the Cross, *The Ascent of Mount Carmel*, in *John of the Cross: Selected Writings*, ed. O. C. D. Kevin Kavanaugh (New York: Paulist Press, 1987), 55.
[6] John of the Cross, *Spiritual Canticle*, 'Stanza III', in *John of the Cross: Selected Writings*, ed. O. C. D. Kevin Kavanaugh (New York: Paulist Press, 1987), 222.

and pursued. So it was when I was on Cadair. Again, unlike the saints, I didn't climb the mountain to find God (I was just looking for an enjoyable couple of days of backpacking), but as I reflected on my two days hiking on the paths that criss-cross Cadair, certain insights began to present themselves to me.

The first was the sense of timelessness I experienced while sitting beside the shore of Llyn Cau, the small lake located in the bowl of Cadair Idris about 1,500 feet above sea level. The geological age that had carved that scene was so far beyond my reckoning that I couldn't imagine the landscape having ever changed. Generations of climbers have ascended to that place, sat at the same spot as I had and admired the same scene. This, in turn, caused me by way of contrast to reflect on the profound sense of history I'd enjoyed earlier that day when I began my walk at an ancient church and a nearby ruined castle. In a single day's walk, I tasted something like eternity in the unchanging landscape surrounding Llyn Cau and rich history in the church and castle at the foot of Cadair. But like worship and creation, eternity and history seemed somehow suited to each other like two old friends sitting together on a park bench. What was I to make of the close camaraderie of ancient historical sites and a place that mocked our notions of time as meaningless?

That was the first and most immediate paradox that drew my attention. Less obviously, I also began to think about the relationship between silence and words. What caused this reflection was the deep quiet of a still night in Cwm Cau, the high valley in which Llyn Cau lies like a blue-green pool in a broken cup. Sheltered from any artificial noise, I was plunged into the uncanny silence of our planet. Take away the sound of the wind and mountains become monstrously silent places – enormous and yet silent as an empty church. This same mountain, however, has been for centuries – probably even millennia – the inspirer of words: it has engendered myths and legends seemingly as old as the mountain itself, inspired poetry to evoke its sublimity and conjured stories told by generations of climbers to impress their friends. What was I to make of this quiet colossus that arouses such a wealth of words?

That was the second paradox on which I later dwelt. The final one begins with the most obvious of observations and common of experiences: Cadair Idris filled me with delight and wonder. That at least came as no surprise. People haul their weary limbs up the steep, craggy paths because they're eager to take in the majestic views across the surrounding mountains and over the Irish Sea. The sublime nature of the mountain is its most apparent trait. Yet, there's nothing unusual about the things that cause such wonder. What's more commonplace than rock, turf, water, cloud, sunshine and trees? We see such things all the time without giving them a second thought. But in places like the slopes and summit of Cadair Idris, everyone without a heart of stone is filled with wonder by those basic elements of the earth. What was I to make of this final paradox of discovering wonder in what's otherwise commonplace?

The more I pondered these three paradoxes in a mountain landscape, the more it seemed to me that somewhere in their midst lay the path to God. Timelessness and time, silence and words, the wonderful and the commonplace: something about those concepts somehow linked my sacramental faith to my love for nature, revealing how they're integrated with the rest of my life. And if this were true, then my journey to the summit of Cadair Idris and back down again was also a pilgrimage towards God and deeper into faith.

These paradoxes also spoke to the profound, melancholic yearning that I've always known and now realize is part of what compels me to walk and explore. My overnight trip didn't satisfy that yearning even for a moment, as though it were a natural drug stupefying an addiction, but it somehow brought that longing out into the open. The short trek may even have explained it. Under the awesome field of stars and again when I stood alone atop the peak of Cadair Idris, I sensed that my deep longing has an object – perhaps in that mountain landscape I had even drawn near to it – and isn't a fantasy or a quirk of my personality. In Welsh, this longing for something we'll probably not find in this life or for a home or love we've forever lost is called *hiraeth*. I experienced *hiraeth* for that part of me that remains exiled, lost to something I still can't quite articulate; I also mourned a world that has in so many ways wandered far from the rich loam of its own humanity.

And yet, in the two days I spent on Cadair Idris, I also experienced a profound peace. Though I had never been there, I felt at home, as though I'd returned from a long journey that was, in fact, my life. It made no sense. I didn't know the place beyond what I'd read on my map. I couldn't even pronounce the names of half the features around me. And yet, as I walked the footpaths or sat by Llyn Cau, I felt deeply at home and at peace. But this didn't really surprise me, because my time spent in the countryside or out in a wilderness almost always feels like a homecoming. And the peace that I feel in that return is like little else. It's what the Welsh call *tangnefedd*: a profound peace that satisfies the soul. Perhaps the yearning and the peace – *hiraeth* and *tangnefedd* – that I experienced are really the final paradox; perhaps they're the paradox that explains all.

If that doesn't make any sense to you, then the only way I can make it clearer is to invite you to join me on my accidental pilgrimage from the little village of Llanfihangel-y-pennant up to the high valley of Cwm Cau and the ridge of Craig Lwyd, then up to the highest peak of Penygadair and back down via an old farm road along the sloping fields of Rhiw Gwredydd. I hope that in so doing, you may find, like me, that this trek is really a pilgrimage of the imagination to God.

PART I

The paradox of eternity and time

FIGURE 1 *Camping in Cwm Cau.*

The knowledge of God is a mountain steep indeed and difficult to climb –
the majority of people scarcely reach its base.
GREGORY OF NYSSA, *Life of Moses* 158

2

Cwm Cau

Timelessness

I sat beside my tent admiring the way the wind tickled the surface of Llyn Cau in the fading autumn sunlight. On three sides of the small mountain lake, rock and turf climbed sharply upwards towards the heights of Penygadair. Behind me, the valley of Cwm Cau dropped away towards the east and south, its centre traced by a rocky stream and its southern edge by the Minffordd Path up which I'd earlier walked. Welsh mountain sheep grazed on its dense, tall grass or stood like sentinels on seemingly unreachable high rocks. Though it had recently rained and much of the ground was boggy, I'd found a ridge of firm turf at the lake's edge and pitched my tent near a scattering of massive rocks deeply pocked by centuries of wind and rain and coated with a thin veneer of pale green and yellow lichen. Cwm Cau is a magical place: the bottom of a colossal cup or seat carved away by glaciers millennia ago when Wales lay under the arctic ice sheet. Cwm Cau gives Cadair Idris its name: Idris's Chair.

After pitching my tent, I pulled on my softshell jacket, grabbed a bottle of ale, and found a dry, comfortable spot on a recumbent rock to enjoy my surroundings. It was a surprisingly warm day for early October in Snowdonia, and so I could sit contentedly drinking my beer with no company other than birds and sheep. I needed the escape: the start of the new term had been busy with lectures to prepare and fresh ordinands to settle into their new life in theological college. The college where I was acting principal was also in the final stages of a complete structural overhaul, a task that I found laborious and disagreeable. Just that morning, too, my wife of nearly eighteen years had informed me of her decision to end our marriage. We had been through much together, including a move to the UK from America, and were still raising my then teenage son. But we'd grown distant over the years. Although I knew its end was approaching, I was too emotionally weary and overworked to try to save our marriage. There was much on my mind as I admired the wind-licked surface of Llyn Cau.

I could hear nothing except the building wind, the occasional frantic flap of rooks swooping from the summit of Cadair Idris, and the regular bleating of sheep. No noise of car or airplane reached my camp. Except for my tent, nothing in reach of my eyes or ears would have been out of place a hundred or even a thousand years ago. Sitting alone, I could easily imagine that time has no meaning in the craggy amphitheatre of Cwm Cau. My view and the sounds that echoed around me were now as they surely must have been ever since sheep were first introduced in the long, forgotten past. What do rocks, the wind, sheep and birds know of our time? 'Eternity has no time. It is itself all time,' Tertullian had written in the third century. Here I could see he was right.

Unlike wild places back home in the States, Cwm Cau has a cosy timeless quality as though all the violent geological forces have conspired to create a perfect place for wonder and peaceful pondering. Except for belligerent bulls, Britain has no predators to threaten: the last bears and wolves were hunted to extinction centuries ago, and the only remaining wildcats prowl in the Scottish Highlands and resemble large tabby cats more than lions. Really, the only two dangers one faces in the patches of British wilderness are unpredictable weather and clumsiness. Of course, these can conspire – one regularly hears accounts of people being blown off mountaintops in strong gales or stumbling off high rocks as they try to inch their way through dense fog. Indeed, once when climbing Snowdon, I stopped for a light meal and a rest in an enshrouding fog blissfully unaware that not 10 feet from me the ground dropped precipitously hundreds of feet down the high cliff of Clogwyn du – I could easily have walked over the edge had I continued a little farther.

But now I was reclining safely on my rock on a lovely October evening with no weather forecasted to trouble me. I could simply drink in my surroundings and let recent stress and anxieties drain away. It is a magical spot. Even better, it's a magical spot that I was fortunate enough to enjoy alone. No other soul disturbed my peaceful reverie. I sat on that rock for over an hour, though I'm not really sure how long it was as my only sense of time was the sun sinking ever nearer to the high ridge of Cadair and the shadows extending ever farther to the east. Gradually, my thoughts and feelings about my life gave way to the deep serenity of my surroundings. Both my past and future couldn't stand long against the powerful *now* of that moment.

Moments like this are one of the reasons why I walk; they're when I'm transported out of myself and, as far as possible, into the eternal now. Moments like this are when I realize how elastic time is and how obsessed with minutes and seconds our frenetic lifestyles force us to be. I'm not convinced the mind was created to cope with precisely measured time without regular periods of mental idleness. Spend a day walking alone in the countryside and you quickly discover that the mind slips into a different mode of consciousness: reflective and yet receptive to what lies around. Without such experiences, I don't know how one can speak meaningfully of eternity or have any sense of what heaven might be like. As contemplatives have long acknowledged, we need to be transported out of ourselves to begin to understand who we are and who God is. Otherwise, we're like caged birds trying to imagine what it's like to fly.

I suppose, though, to notice Cwm Cau's timeless personality, I had to ignore the ticking clock. The unchanging landscape was transformed into something more than just a pleasant scene only when I simply enjoyed it with reverent delight. Had I kept checking my watch or been pressed by an engagement, I wouldn't have recognized the timeless quality of the valley or been absorbed by the surrounding scene. I had to settle into a patient receptivity, letting go of everything that pressed on me – in fact, I had to let go of myself. But Cwm Cau's beauty seduced me and wrapped itself around my senses in a deep embrace without my ever being conscious of it happening. I hadn't come in search of the mountain's timelessness, but having encountered it, I couldn't remain impassive.

Moreover, Cwm Cau isn't just any place. Even now, I can see with my mind's eye the shape of the lake, the features of the rocks scattered around it and the way the light plays on the high cliffs. I can picture the sheep perched precariously up and down the steep slopes and know that even now, in the cold driving rain on the day I'm writing this sentence, they're still there. I can see the birds playing in the air currents and the pools of water blackened by the peaty earth among the tall moor-grass. All these and many more things imbue Cwm Cau with personality. It *feels* a particular way – as distinct as any human personality.

Yes, aspects of the Cwm Cau remind me of elsewhere – Llyn Bochlwyd below Glyder Fach or Llyn y Gadair on just the other side of Cadair spring to mind – but that's no different than people I know who remind me of each other. I can tell you where each of the hundreds of hiking photos on my hard drive was taken without any prompts – even those of fields dotted with grazing sheep that look much the same. Anyone who has taken to trekking in the wilderness or countryside knows that each place has its own character, its own irreducible personality: sights, sounds, the feel of the air, the smell of earth and plants and, most of all, the way all these interweave to imprint themselves on a receptive and perceptive mind, to make one locale unique from another.

They can even become akin to friends. There are places I yearn to visit at particular times of the year. On these occasions, just going outdoors isn't enough; I want to visit the place that's calling to me and to spend time in its company. That might be as large as the summits of the Brecon Beacons or as small as a stretch of track that lies beneath a row of ancient oaks alongside a field of ripe barley. Part of their friendship, however, is that I can depend on their personality. I know that when I return, the place will be unchanged and that our acquaintance, as it were, can resume where we left off. I was recently reminded of the importance of this dependable sameness when I took my wife to a spot where I once walked regularly only to find that the old track had been widened and paved for heavy vehicles. That one change dispelled the place's charm. It felt tragic, like an injury that causes a friend's personality to worsen. I've not returned since.

So long as natural landscapes are left alone, their personality is as changeless as the earth – we simply can't comprehend the deep geological and climatic periods to which they're subject. From our vantage, natural landscapes seem to remain the same, generation after generation after generation. Seasons pass along them like moods, making them seem different for a spell without actually altering their underlying character. Perhaps that's why we turn to weather to describe our moods: the warm sunshine of happiness, the frost of indifference or depression, and the storms of anger. Our language acknowledges that these changes don't really impact the underlying topography of our personalities. Like the land, we remain unaltered.

Of course, the timelessness of our landscapes is illusory. Geologists are fond of reminding people that environments are in constant flux. Were I to somehow observe landscapes from a cosmic perspective, they would seem like fluid, flowing from one form into another. Since the earth first solidified into its familiar sphere, much has altered: continents have drifted, mountains have risen and worn away, seas have expanded and receded, and species of flora and fauna have flourished and vanished. Millions of years ago (or so I'm told), Cadair Idris lay alongside Canada and Greenland. In fact, according to Robert Moor's *On Trails: An Exploration*, these mountains were once part of the same range as the Appalachians where I used to walk and camp in North Carolina.[1] Much more recently, as late as the Middle Ages, most of the slopes around me were wooded with oak, hazel, and alder and other trees that could cling on through frequent gales.[2] But I can't really adopt a cosmic viewpoint; I can't really even imagine it. The calendar to which Cadair Idris and all wildernesses are subject is too sprawling for my short-sighted perspective. That's part of their beauty.

Because such places are so immeasurably ancient, changing at an imperceptibly slow pace, I'm disposed towards the eternal whenever I consciously relate to them. They elongate my sense of time, pressing my own understanding of past-present-future far beyond breaking point. They're vastly more ancient than any concept I have of being old, will be around aeons beyond any hopes and fears I have about the future, and have been and will be present throughout human history to anyone who visits them. Unless we've destroyed ourselves before then, men and women a thousand even ten thousand years hence will come to Cwm Cau to admire the same landscape as I; perhaps they'll even pitch a tent and enjoy a beer sitting on the same rock that served as my seat. As a historian, I frequently reflect on the passage of time. But the sum of all human time is nothing more than the present in the elongated lifespan of Cadair Idris. What's a few thousand years in

---

[1]See Robert Moor, *On Trails: An Exploration* (London: Autumn Press, 2016).
[2]Peter Rhind and Margaret Jones, 'The Vegetation History of Snowdonia since the Late Glacial Period', *Field Studies* 10 (2003): 539–52.

comparison to 500 million? As Elizabeth in *Pride and Prejudice* declares, 'What are men to rocks and mountains?' To Cadair Idris, the thirty thousand years separating the first humans in Wales from me are as an instant.

-o0o-

I find this combination of timelessness and personality compelling because they appear contradictory. Human personalities are full of change, adapting to the people and circumstances that affect them. As Plato recognized long ago, to exist in this world is to be in constant motion, never staying still for a moment: thoughts flow from one to another, the positions of our bodies shift, our hearts expand and contract, emotions ebb and flow, new ideas take hold as old ones give way, and on and on. Our experiences in life change us enormously over time for the better and the worse. To be alive is to be ever changing; even death fails to stop this activity until, I suppose, we have decayed to nothing. '[H]ere below to live is to change', wrote John Henry Newman, 'and to be perfect is to have changed often.'[3] For us, time and personality are inextricably bound together. Time is marked in our lives by the changes we embrace, endure and regret.

If that's the case, then how can something be personal without ever changing? Timelessness implies changelessness, since to change from one thing into another is to invoke a *then* and *now*, a *before* and *after*. It seems impossible for us to imagine an unchanging personality, a thing that relates to us and the world without ever being affected by it. And yet, I have encountered both timelessness and personality in places like Cwm Cau. Except at a theoretical level, I can't imagine a *before* and *after* when it comes to such places: they never change unless by cataclysm or some act of human perversity. They could take Elizabeth I's motto as their own: *semper eadem*, always the same. And yet, they have personalities as distinct from other places as we have from each other. They are both timeless and companionable.

Many theologians would disagree with me. The conviction that something can't be both personal and changeless has been central

---

[3]John Henry Newman, *An Essay on the Development of Christian Doctrine* (London: James Toovey, 1845), 39.

to a powerful strand of Christian thought since the mid-twentieth century. According to this argument, portraying God as timeless makes him impersonal and distant, especially from the pain and suffering of our world. For God to be personal – one who relates not only to creation as a whole but also to each one of us – he must be able to interact. He must, in fact, be able to suffer alongside us. How can an unchanging, timeless Deity respond to our prayers, which are so very often of the moment, focused exquisitely on others or ourselves in the anguish of present suffering? As Dietrich Bonhoeffer wrote, 'The Bible directs people toward the powerlessness and the suffering of God; only the suffering God can help.'[4]

The Bible, of course, is full of examples of God responding immediately to human activity: speaking with people like Moses, responding to prayers and even getting angry or being pleased. The Old Testament constantly portrays a God infuriated with his people, deeply upset by their lack of faithfulness. All these suggest that God can be affected by his creation – by us humans – and that he responds directly to it, which implies, too, that he changes. In fact, Exod. 32.14 and Numbers 14 give two accounts when Moses successfully implored God to change his mind and spare the people he had led out of bondage from Egypt.

On the other hand, James says in his epistle that in God there's 'no variation or shadow due to change' (Jam. 1.17), and Paul assures us that 'Jesus Christ is the same yesterday and today and forever' (Rom. 11.29). Until the twentieth century, Christian theologians by and large assumed that God is impassible, unaffected by anything that happens in his creation. In the words of the great hymn:

To all, life Thou givest, to both great and small,
in all life Thou livest, the true life of all;
we blossom and flourish as leaves on the tree,
and wither and perish, but naught changeth Thee.

He who is both perfect and eternal can't change since to do so implies both time and imperfection – eternity permits no variation,

---

[4]Dietrich Bonhoeffer, *Letters and Papers from Prison* (Minneapolis: Fortress Press, 2010), 479.

no *befores* and *afters*, since these would make the eternal intolerable
– like being stuck endlessly on hold.

But if God *is* unchanging, doesn't this imply that he's distant and
unable to interact with his constantly changing creation? How can
anything be personal if it doesn't react and respond? To put this
question pointedly: If God can't feel compassion (which means to
suffer alongside the suffering), then how can he be a God of love?
The great German theologian Jürgen Moltmann states the obvious
answer:

> A God who cannot suffer is poorer than any man. For a God
> who is incapable of suffering is a being who cannot be involved.
> Suffering and injustice do not affect him. And because he is
> so completely insensitive, he cannot be affected or shaken by
> anything. He cannot weep, for he has no tears. But the one who
> cannot suffer cannot love either. So he is also a loveless being.[5]

An unchanging God would seem to be a loveless God. With all
the horrors of the twentieth century in mind, Moltmann so wanted
to keep hold of the belief that 'God is love' that he takes the only
course he sees open to him: to say that God is deeply affected by all
he created and redeemed.

But what I discovered perched on my rock in Cwm Cau is
that timelessness can be intensely personal. Nothing about the
landscape seemed foreign or distant. Indeed, its very timelessness
and *dependable* changelessness are part of Cwm Cau's strong
attraction. I suppose my encounter with such incredibly ancient
landscapes is why I've never been troubled by the idea of a timeless,
unchanging God. Spend time in the wilderness or return to the same
spot after a space of time and you'll observe that there need be no
contradiction between timelessness and personality. The discovery
that a changeless landscape becomes intensely personal when
it plays on our affections teaches our imaginations to see how a
timeless God can also be personal. I know without a shadow of a
doubt that if I have the good fortune to return to Cwm Cau twenty

---

[5]Jürgen Moltmann, *Crucified God: The Cross of Christ as the Foundation and Criticism of Christian Theology* (London: SCM Press, 1974), 222.

years from now, I'll encounter an old friend who has remained unchanged. I may even feel young in that reunion.

Someone might respond, I know, that this is hardly a rational argument and doesn't even begin to answer the theological inconsistencies and ethical problems that the timeless immutability of God raises. Their question to me might be: 'Did Cwm Cau love me back?' And my reply would have to be 'no'. The feelings I had when reflecting on my surroundings were all within me. They were a romantic sensibility, a fancy that some personality quirk disposed me to entertain. Charming perhaps, but certainly not real. Immanuel Kant termed this a subjective 'feeling' of the sublime: the feeling of dread, wonder or delight that magnificent landscapes can produce in us. To say that Cwm Cau is wonderful is just a shorthand way of saying that I experienced the sensation of wonder when I visited that place of towering rock. I may have delighted in the lake, the heights, the sheep and the diving rooks, but none of them took much notice of me. They certainly didn't delight in me. And so, rationally, I should admit that a personal God can't be timeless and immutable or else accept that an unchanging God can't be bothered much with me no matter how much I might love him. Wasn't Cwm Cau really teaching me that I can love and be transformed by that which doesn't know or love me back?

That lesson isn't in itself altogether worthless. It is, in fact, not far from the philosophy of the Neoplatonists, who believed that a philosophical love for the utterly transcendent divine is the pathway to eternal life. Places like Cwm Cau teach us that we can fall in love with things that aren't oriented towards us personally. I can relate to something and by it be changed for better or worse without any reciprocity whatsoever. I can't demand a fair exchange between myself and a sublime view; there's no bartering with nature. All I can do is try to remain deliberately impervious to its beauty or allow it to strum my affections like skilled fingers on the strings of a harp. As strange as it sounds, I can be wooed by that which doesn't even know or care that I exist.

But that's precisely the point: to be captivated by such places is to be drawn out of my small self into something immeasurably larger. We so easily become self-absorbed, believing that something's worth is determined by how it affects or responds to us; it must be useful or responsive to be of value. But what if our deepest loves are invoked by those things that are impervious to our will? Perhaps our soul's well-being requires that we experience the overthrow of our self-regard: the absorption of ourselves into something else, especially into something we perceive to be nobler and higher than ourselves. Philosophers have identified that nobler thing as transcendent beauty.

I begin now to get ahead of myself and need to return to the question at hand. As much as I may have felt a timeless personality about Cwm Cau, it would be ridiculous to suggest it loved me. But I think there's a third way to understand what Cwm Cau taught me about God: I can embrace paradox.

To follow what I mean, you must first understand that while Catholicism has always respected rational argument (just read Anselm or Aquinas), it hasn't done so to the exclusion of our other faculties or ways of engaging with the world. Christianity's embrace of mystery and paradox pushes us beyond the rational towards an awareness – an appreciation even – of the fundamental unknowableness of the cosmos. If we believe that we can examine, understand and explain everything, then we also tend to assume that everything is knowable, even measurable. Christianity's paradoxes mock this idea: a Virgin gives birth, God becomes man, the earthly is utterly united with the divine, the eternal enters the temporal, the almighty God is a babe in Bethlehem, and the changeless responds to his ever-changing creation.

> How could the Eternal do a temporal act,
> The Infinite become a finite fact?
> Nothing can save us that is possible:
> We who must die demand a miracle.[6]

If we accept the idea that the eternal and infinite can enter a fixed moment in our time and become a historical fact (that is, that God became man), then there's almost no absurdity we can't swallow. These beliefs demand something from us: they insist that we should not just tolerate mystery, we should also revel in it.

Catholicism has usually sought to balance rationality with ideas such as affection, delight and mystery, which remind us that much of life can't be contained within our logical explanations. My contemplation of Cwm Cau was not, in fact, a rational endeavour. The lessons it taught me about the timelessness of God weren't rational ones – the

---

[6]W. H. Auden, *For the Time Being: A Christmas Oratorio*, 'Advent', III (Princeton: Princeton University Press, 2013), 8.

landscape engaged my affections, my imagination, and drew out of me a deep yearning. But none of these *explained* the changelessness and timelessness of God; I didn't gain any information from the experience. What Cwm Cau did offer was a taste of something *like* eternity – but it offered that taste to the palate of my imagination rather than the observation of my reason. The magnificent scenery of Cwm Cau may not have responded to my affection in a personal way; nevertheless, it disposed me towards imagining something or someone that can. The leap isn't far from a timeless landscape that acts upon my deepest affections to a timeless God who acts upon my deepest affections and paradoxically *responds to them*.

Experience expanded my imagination. Had I never encountered the comfortable companionship of an unchanging landscape, then I suppose I might have associated both changelessness and timelessness with something like a waiting room in a sterile clinic with canned music, unvaried décor and what seems like the same people always waiting alongside me. Likewise, I probably would have seen no possibility for an unchanging God to avoid being cold, heartless. The experience of places like Cwm Cau, however, means that I don't have to worry about such negative connotations: I may never find convincing arguments for the timeless immutability of God, but I also don't need to. Because of my wilderness experiences, I associate the idea of timelessness with something natural (rather than artificial), cosy, personal and with something that feels akin to *home*. Is not the mysterious combination of the unchanging and the deeply personal a key element of what we call home?

So, Cwm Cau spoke to my imagination and my affections. There are many such places for me: the reed-fragrant beaches of the Carolinas, the scrub pine forest near the Loxahatchee in Florida, Ivestor Gap in the Shining Rock Wilderness, an otherwise non-descript slope in the Cotswolds, Glyder Fach and Fan Fawr on a late autumn's evening (to name but a few). Such places have laid powerful claim to my loyalty by their combination of beauty and timelessness. Each has unstintingly imparted its gift to me simply by its timeless beauty. And the nature of their gift is the shaping and expansion of my imagination, of the way I view and understand the reality in which I've been placed. Their gift is far more powerful than any argument because they have laid claim to my deepest loyalties.

-o0o-

Such places have also shown me that I can trust their lessons as much as those of the wise. There is a wisdom of man and a wisdom of the earth. Such places have taught me that I can *trust the earth;* unlike us, the earth is both honest and without pretence. It doesn't seek to fool us and is free from our self-delusions. Perhaps our problem lies in desire. We don't just believe things; we *want* to believe them, too. We want things to be a certain way. And we want others to see them as we do. Often, our arguments, our own statements, are compromised by our needs and desires – we believe them to be true because we want them to be true. For us, the line between desire and truth is usually impossible to trace. The earth is free of that and thus its lessons are more candid.

Christ described his Kingdom with very earthy parables: he used seeds, lost sheep, pearls, wheat and tares, grapevines and a fig tree to teach us about the Father and himself. He invited us to consider the lilies and the birds, and he suggested that God loves his creation so intimately that he's aware of even a sparrow's fall. It seems to me that in so doing Christ encourages us to see creation as a parable that reveals something of God. The first chapter of Romans certainly suggests that God is to be seen everywhere in creation but that we're often too stupid or blind to find him: 'For what can be known about God is plain to them, because God has shown it to them. Ever since the creation of the world his eternal power and divine nature, invisible though they are, have been understood and seen through the things he has made' (Rom. 1.19-20). All created things are parables in potential.

Many of the greatest Christian thinkers have found God's footprints in creation. A good example of this comes from Augustine's *Confessions*:

What is the object of my love? I asked the earth and it said, 'It is not I.' I asked all that is in it; they made the same confession. I asked the sea, the deeps, the living creatures that creep, and they responded: 'We are not your God look beyond us.' I asked the breezes that blow and the entire air with its inhabitants said: 'Anazimenes was mistaken; I am not God.' I asked heaven, sun, moon and stars; they said, 'Nor are we the God whom you seek.' And I said to all things in my external environment: 'Tell me of my God who you are not, tell me something about him.' And with a great voice they cried out: 'He made us.' My question was the attention I gave to them, and their response was their beauty.[7]

What they all seem to be saying, even if some of them didn't realize it, is *trust the earth*. Unlike us, the earth is without deceit, though we may draw wrong conclusions from what we find there. But I think we're less likely to misinterpret creation when in the countryside and wilderness than in our built spaces. Out there away from our artificial environments we can, with discernment, encounter God like Adam and Eve, Jacob, Moses and Elijah did.

Notice, however, that I say *encounter* rather than *explain* God. Perhaps it would be better to say *portray* or *point towards* God. Jesus didn't devise his teachings about the Father from his thoughtful observation of seeds and errant sheep. It's not as if he saw a shepherd searching for a lost sheep and stopped to ponder what that might teach him about the Father. Augustine didn't begin with his encounter with natural beauty and then extrapolate to his beliefs about God, as though he could have discovered the doctrines of the creed by his questions. Creation offers us beauty, wonder and many other things; it doesn't offer us an explanation beyond itself. Science turns to nature for explanations. It's well suited for answering the questions of geologists, biologists and climatologists. Ask nature to explain God and its response is simply to continue being nature. But ask nature to show us something about God, to point us towards him in all his mystery, to dispose us towards accepting what has been revealed, and it leaps to a response.

How does it do this? I think it's partly by how nature tests the fruits of the beliefs we cherish. For example, Rom. 8.18-35 speaks of creation yearning for freedom from death and decay, which only comes through our redemption; Scripture also teaches that we were created in the first place to tend the earth, suggesting that humanity's truest vocation is really to be earth's gardeners. Doesn't climate change, the acidification of our seas, the destruction of fish stock, and mass extinction all suggest that nature knows these teachings to be true? The scientific utilitarianism and reductionism that allowed us to think that everything should be subject to the

---

[7]Augustine, *Confessions*, trans. Henry Chadwick (Oxford: Oxford University Press, 1992), 10.6.

human will have led us to mass environmental degradation. The belief that humankind stands apart from, rather than within and alongside, the rest of creation has quickly led to the Anthropocene: a period of mass extinction on the same scale as the meteor strike that killed the dinosaurs. Nature's angry response should teach us how false our present-day beliefs about humanity are and that we need to get back to our true vocation. The cry of a suffering planet may not explain God or demonstrate our need to worship him, but it does increasingly dispose us towards accepting our human vocation to be good stewards.

In other words, there should be a congeniality between our religious beliefs and the creation in which we live. Our gaze towards heaven shouldn't be so fixed that we neglect the earth. We can't long for heaven without remembering Eden. If our reading of the Bible produces an adversarial relationship between the earth and us, then we know we've read badly. If our reading of the Bible causes us to neglect creation, then we know we need to read again. Nature proclaims God and seeks to correct our wilful heresies. My beliefs about God the Creator, the Incarnation, Death and Resurrection of his Son, and about human redemption may arise from the church's interpretation of Scripture, but they're confirmed by their congeniality with the earth. One taste of spring was sufficient for me to know deep down that Christ has been raised from the dead and one glimpse of nature's reclamation of a disused industrial site that redemption is always possible.

My treks into changeless wildernesses like Cwm Cau disposed me towards accepting what I'd been taught about God's own timelessness. Those treks have taught me that there's no contradiction between the timeless and the personal, that even within creation my deepest affections can be engaged by that which seems changeless. Having accepted that teaching, I can now see signs of divine immutability wherever I go. God is timeless; God is personal. How do I know? Because he created places like Cwm Cau that are also timeless and personal. And having encountered him in such places, I can't forget him soon. That's the nature of God as Jacob discovered in his own wilderness. Moreover, thanks to places like Cwm Cau, I'm convinced that should I reach heaven, I'll find it deeply familiar, as though it had been lurking all along amid and behind the beautiful places I've visited.

How else will I know it as home?

3

Dysynni Valley

Thick time

Earlier on the same day that I sat by Llyn Cau pondering God's timelessness, I began my walk in the little village of Llanfihangel-y-pennant at the top of the Dysynni Valley. The village contains a single-aisled, medieval church dedicated to St Michael the Archangel, a few farms scattered among hedged fields and along hillsides, and a long, white farmhouse, ancient in origin, that had been divided into a couple of cottages. There was little to give the settlement shape except for the topography and the Afon Cader that runs through the centre of the parish. I saw no village green, and there were certainly no shops; even the church sat in splendid isolation, largely invisible to the rest of the village behind tall hedgerows of hawthorn.

As I pulled into the car park where I planned to leave my car, sombrely dressed locals made their way quietly to the church for a funeral, as no doubt people have done for more than seven hundred years. A Church in Wales lay reader dressed in black cassock, white surplice and cerulean scarf greeted them beneath an arched stone gateway into the churchyard. Few came by car, most walking from the nearby homes and farms that comprise the village. The deceased must have been local. I briefly considered introducing myself to the reader – at the time I was the acting principal of the theological college that trained most clergy and many lay readers in Wales – but opted, instead, to remain anonymous. She undoubtedly had other things on her mind at that moment. So, I sat in my car watching the locals walk in solemn packs towards the church and thought about all the baptisms, weddings and funerals that humble church has hosted over the centuries.

The eulogist must have been unusually succinct because by the time I'd eaten my lunch and prepared my backpack for the trek up Cadair Idris, the villagers had started to emerge from the church and en masse to retrace their steps up the village lane, I supposed to a reception at the house of the deceased or their close family. After they'd departed, I decided to nip into the church to look around. Like many Welsh churches there wasn't a great deal to see. The church is plain and unadorned with two rows of old wooden pews, a narrow sanctuary demarcated by a communion rail with a low pulpit and a side vestry containing a small museum that exhibits the local history. At the rear of the church stands a stone, rectangular font that apparently dates to the twelfth or thirteenth century, probably before the church itself was built. I love these ancient, humble Welsh churches. They rarely feature in colourful books of grand Gothic churches like the wool churches that dot the Cotswolds and East Anglia. But they have their own modest charm and strike me as somehow more of the people and less of the local grandees.

One shouldn't be fooled by St Michael's modesty. As the tiny museum was eager to inform visitors, the church is associated with Mary Jones, a teenage girl who in 1800 walked 26 miles across the mountains to Bala to fetch a copy of the Bible in her native Welsh. Her devotion (not to mention endurance) inspired the great Thomas Charles to establish the Bible Society, which has been distributing Bibles and encouraging its study worldwide ever since. Although Mary Jones was a member of the strict and stern Calvinistic Methodism (watch the Hugh Grant film *The Englishman Who Went Up a Hill But Came Down a Mountain* to get a picture of what this was like), the Anglican churchyard contains the graves of her parents and is happy to look past denominational niceties to commemorate her life. Thus, through the piety of a poor Welsh teenage girl, the little village nestled among the remote hills of Snowdonia has touched the lives of countless people from around the globe. I later discovered in the village a memorial erected in her honour that reads in both Welsh and English:

> In memory of Mary Jones, who in
> The year 1800, at the age of 16 walked

From here to Bala, to procure from the
Revd Thomas Charles, B.A.
A copy of the Welsh Bible. This incident
Was the occasion of the formation of
The British and Foreign Bible Society.
Erected by the Sunday Schools of Merioneth.

Yet, Llanfihangel-y-pennant is not so peculiar – one of the aspects of Britain I love dearly is how often one finds forgotten places whose impact on the world has been formidable.

I saw on my OS map that just up the road, and not far from a path that would take me where I needed to go, stands Castell-y-Bere. According to my copy of Plantagenet Somerset Fry's classic *Castles of the British Isles*, Castell-y-Bere 'was a native Welsh castle raised on a spur of land in the shadow of Cadair Idris'.[1] That about sums up the place. It's now a ruinous heap astride a rocky knoll overlooking the fields and hedges that divide up the valley. It was built around 1221 by Llywelyn Fawr, the mighty Welsh Prince of Wales who caused trouble for King John, his much more benign son Henry III and not a few Anglo-Norman Marcher Lords. It must have been an impressive piece of masonry in its day, especially for the relatively poor Welsh princes. Like other Welsh fortresses, however, it was no match for the English army of Edward I, which captured it in 1283 in the campaign that brought Welsh independence to an end. Indeed, it was the last Welsh castle to fall to that 'great and terrible' king. Afterwards, attempts were made to refurbish and make it the focus of a new town, but all it managed to produce was the little village I'd just left.

Today, its crumbling walls have almost melted back into the natural rock and ancient wood so that now all three seem perfectly suited to each other. Strange to think that the place was a working castle for less than seventy years and only ever saw one siege at which it was taken; for the past almost 800 years, it has slowly crumbled away under the dual assault of wet Welsh winters and local farmers filching dressed stone for their own homes and boundary walls.

---

[1]Plantagenet Somerset Fry, *Castles of the British Isles* (New York: Dorset Press, 1990), 338.

I didn't have long to spend at the site, but I couldn't resist a short visit. It's a striking and largely unknown place with magnificent views over the trees of the valley and surrounding mountains. King Edward I may have conquered the fort, but he certainly couldn't have crept up on it. What must it have been like for the small Welsh garrison to watch their doom, in the guise of English knights and foot soldiers, approaching up the valley? They must have known their fate long before the siege engines of the accursed *Saes* had arrived.

I later discovered, however, that one part of the castle does remain in use: the baptismal font. Apparently, the old font I'd seen in the parish church originally stood in the castle chapel (or so some historians think). How wonderful that the one part of the castle to endure intact is a small stone font in which generations of infants have been sacramentally washed and given entry into the Body of Christ. In the end, a place built for warfare and to mete out pain and death to invaders only really managed to be useful by bequeathing a font in which eight hundred years of local children have received new life in Christ. History often offers such ironies in hindsight.

A glance at my map suggested I could easily spend an entire day visiting nearby standing stones, cairns and pre-Roman forts. If Castell-y-Bere was already ancient by the time Mary Jones made her trek to Bala, then some of these other sites made the castle seem positively newfangled: a cairn dating back to the Bronze Age, a fort atop the splendid Craig yr Aderyn dating back to before Roman times and a forlorn standing stone stuck in a hedge that was erected God only knows when. If time has no meaning at the shore of Llyn Cau, here in the valley it permeates everything.

This is *thick time* where the generations overlap and one age speaks to another. In a single sweep of my vision, I could take in two thousand years of human history bottled up in a small valley in west Wales. To live among layers of history is a remarkable experience. Archaeologists determine much in their digs from the stratigraphy of the soil: the different strata of earth that reveal how a site developed over time. Their work reminds us that the earth itself contains memory and that history can be read in more than books. Places like the Dysynni Valley suggest that communities and their landscape are likewise stratigraphic. The layers of history are visible for anyone to see. People were around a few thousand years ago to erect their cairns on the mountains, their descendants built a fort on Craig yr Aderyn when there were rumours of the approaching Roman eagle, and their descendants watched as a Castell-y-Bere was built and destroyed. Perhaps their blood ran in the veins of Mary Jones and continues to do so in some of the local residents today. The span of time that separates these people of different ages is contracted by the fact that one can still visit each site – their memory, or the faintest echo of it, is made present in the landscape they now share.

Whatever the period, the inhabitants of Llanfihangel-y-pennant have lived with these ancient sites alongside their own old homes and farmsteads. A local historian could write a learned treatise charting the long history of the valley, but that wouldn't capture its thick time. I suppose one would need to grow up and live in the valley to have a chance of knowing that time. It can really be known only from the inside. It's the kind of historical wisdom that's written into people's imagination over generations and in the company of everything else that makes a place one's home: the people, the local features, the way the landscape responds to the seasons, the great and small events that happen or are reported over time and the stories handed down from one generation to another. It's the sense of history one can develop only by relating continually to a place – it requires stability and constancy, a willingness to set down roots and remain fixed long enough to grow familiar – in effect, to belong to the landscape as much as the old buildings and the enduring natural features do.

An example of this can be found on Carreg yr Enwau, a rock that lies half buried in the spongey peat near one of the paths up Cadair Idris. On it are inscribed names, the earliest of which dates back to the seventeenth century. They're mostly of shepherds who have worked for generations on the slopes, tending their flocks in a nearly unchanging practice that links those of the present to their most distant forebears. Here's memory actually inscribed in stone: what it must be like for a local shepherd to sit by that rock on a wet, foggy day, his sheep bleating around him and his rubber wellies planted on the black earth he has known his entire life! It's no wonder that in an interview with S4C (a Welsh television channel) many of them said they wouldn't leave the valley for all the money in the world.

This is the kind of history that many of us today don't know because modernity has uprooted us. Our success stories invariably involve the protagonists escaping places like the Dysynni Valley to make something of themselves in the modern world. This is the common theme of books and films from *Billy Elliott* to *Hillbilly Elegy*. Moreover, we move too often to have a profound familiarity with the land and its history. Late modernity has made many of us nomads with routines and habits that can be transported almost anywhere more easily than Bedouins can pack their camels and horses to move to new grazing grounds. Or thanks to TVs, comfortable houses and cars, we can live in a place our entire life and not actually ever inhabit it. We can relate to the place where we live like two people sharing a flat but never stopping to speak to each other or like a room full of strangers whose faces are only ever turned towards their smartphones.

I have sadly experienced both of these symptoms of modernity. I'm a restless soul, probably a necessary attribute for someone who enjoys walking as much as I do. But that quality combined with circumstances often out of my control has led so far to a life of constant uprooting. I have lived all over: South Carolina, Wisconsin, Ohio, three different homes in Florida, two in Virginia, another two in North Carolina and three in Maryland. Since moving to Britain in 2008, I have lived in houses near Durham with her magnificent cathedral, twice in or near Oxford, in two homes near Cardiff in Wales, and now in Brecon. That works out to less than three years in each home over the course of my entire life. I'm a man without a home; there's nowhere for me to return to, to gather myself up, and reconnect with the place that formed me. Life has made me a drifter.

At the same time, because of the frequency of those moves, I think I've learned to appreciate places quickly. I don't just live somewhere, I tend to dive deeply into it, learning its history and exploring its nooks and crannies. I suppose that makes me promiscuous, transferring my affections from one place to another like a womanizer his many *amours*, remaining attentive and besotted only with the place I currently call home. In truth, though, I remain very much in love with most of the places where I've lived – especially during the past twenty years – and return to them regularly by imagination if not by foot.

Yet, because I am promiscuous, I also recognize that I don't really know any of the places I've called home. Again, like a fickle lover, I haven't remained long enough to know them intimately. I haven't been faithful and constant, so I am like someone who has enjoyed many lovers but never married; I've savoured their charms without ever pledging my troth. The lack of stability has kept me from the deepest knowledge one can have for the other, which is a true and abiding love anchored by *presence*. And so, for all my antiquated ideas, I am in this respect thoroughly modern.

In his book, *Life is a Miracle*, Wendell Berry describes what living in places like the Dysynni Valley provides:

> No human being has ever known, let alone imagined, the entire planet. And even in an age of 'world travel', none of us lives on the entire planet; in fact, owing to so much mobility, a lot of people . . . don't live anywhere. But if we are to know any part of the planet intimately, particularly, precisely, and with affection, then we must live somewhere in particular for a long time. We must be able to call up to the mind's eye by name a lot of local places, people, creatures, and things.
>
> One of the most significant costs of the economic destruction of farm populations is the loss of local memory, local history, and local names. Field names for instance, even such colorless names as 'the front field' and 'the back field' are vital signs of a culture.[2]

Thick-history is always known locally and through intimate familiarity. It can't be captured in any guidebook or history, and it eludes most tourists and even walkers. It underpins the local culture of the insiders – it's their history and not that of outsiders.

Although Berry was thinking about his own home in Kentucky, his mention of field names is striking in the context of Llanfihangel-y-pennant. There, scholars have been studying the names of the surrounding hills to get a better understanding of the local history. The field names carry memories. Take, for example, one called Palmant Foty. With a little etymological work, scholars can confidently say that the field name means something like a 'cottage on a pavement' or words to that effect. Sure enough, if you look carefully, you can see the rocky, rectangular outline of what must have been a small hovel: once the shelter for herders who brought cattle up from the valley to this field to feed on the lush, summer grass. In the name of a field is preserved a medieval practice now otherwise lost. The same is true for many of the other field names around it. Indeed, in Wales much of the land's history has been written into the landscape, the most durable material in the face of a dominant English culture.

Ever since I was a child, I've been drawn powerfully to places of thick-history. Perhaps because I spent much of my childhood in South

---

[2]Wendell Berry, *Life Is a Miracle: An Essay against Modern Superstition* (Berkeley: Counterpoint, 2000), 138.

Florida where there are few traces of history, I became sensitive to thick-history whenever I encountered it. Once, upon seeing a historical marker for a schoolhouse built in Palm Beach County during the early twentieth century, my Yorkshire grandmother sniffed in disgust and exclaimed, 'That must make me *pre*historic.' So much of America is like that: two-dimensional in its relationship with the landscape and its own heritage. We Americans are too quick to tear down old buildings or turn them into museums and tourist attractions. Too much of our history came after trains and automobiles had begun to make towns uniform. What does a shopping mall or a fast-food restaurant care about its location other than its accessibility to cars?

My own upbringing in two-dimensional landscapes has made me appreciate those places clearly marked by the third dimension of time. That's why, I think, I can almost feel the ghosts in places that have been allowed to age and decay. I'll more happily visit the overgrown and isolated wreck of an old farmhouse than a great stately home or reconstructed castle. I once visited a National Trust home and was more mesmerized by the fields still undulating with medieval ridges and furrows than I was by the dressed-up building itself. In the soil I could see the work of generations of farmworkers – people who once tilled those fields had heard reports of the death of kings, the arrival of the Black Death and (much to their own misfortune) the coming enclosures that robbed them of their livelihood. The same was true, of course, of those who had lived within the walls of the old manor house, but for me, at least, the well-intentioned work of the National Trust in preserving the home had also banished its ghosts.

My first proper experience of living amid thick time was during my brief stint as vicar of three rural villages in north Oxfordshire. The thick-history there impressed me directly in part through their buildings, old fields and ancient tracks. Their parish churches, for example, contain fabric and monuments that continually put me in the company of generations past. I could see my predecessors listed (with a few gaps) back to the high Middle Ages, with dates suggesting that the Black Death may have carried off some and Cromwell's Commonwealth others. I could reflect on memorials to the fallen in the two world wars and use items and furniture donated by people from the Elizabethan period to the present. At Christmas and Easter, I communicated the faithful using a sixteenth-century chalice and paten from which parishioners have received the Body and Blood of Christ for over four hundred years. Are there any other buildings like parish churches that are so soaked in local history? In them people have been bringing their joys and sorrows for longer than any of us can really imagine. They're drenched in the prayers of commonplace people who have come to God with their commonplace concerns, hopes and prejudices. They are the quintessential and now too-neglected shrines to the human condition in the presence of God.

But what captured my imagination as much as the buildings were the stories of the old residents of the villages. Not many are left now, but those who remained when I lived there enjoyed recounting their experiences of life in the villages before farm machinery and commuting by car changed everything. Many of their old local customs had been tied to the agricultural year and had therefore remained much as they had been since time immemorial. I felt a pang of melancholy when one old farmer, who had been forced to sell up years before, reminisced about his old life and what the village was once like when almost everyone had to pitch in to help with sowing, cultivating and harvesting the land. We forget how isolated rural villages once were. Compared to the present village I then knew, dominated by retirees and commuters to London and Oxford, the village of yesteryear had been a large family: undoubtedly full of gossip, feuds and small-mindedness but also where people knew they belonged. How little happens today in such villages to tie the people with the heritage of their own homes.

I know I now risk sliding into romanticism, evoking with my imagination the same nostalgia as the BBC with their period dramas. From a certain perspective, part of our problem with engaging with thick-history is that we invariably surrender to a sentimentalism that's no more faithful to the actual past than the museums I've criticized. But that's only human, isn't it? We do the same with our lovers, parents and children. Reality and our perception of that reality are rarely the same. We aren't machines but flesh-blood-and-soul people who experience, interpret, retell, revise, forget and improvise our way through life. Our sentimental attachments reveal our truest loyalties and affections. How would you describe the people you love most? Objectively? I doubt it. The old American satirist Ambrose Bierce in his wickedly funny *The Devil's Dictionary* defined a saint as 'a dead sinner revised and edited'. 'Revised and edited' are how all our deepest connections emerge from our hearts and minds. And that process of revising reveals to others how our relationships with particular people and places have fashioned us.

We manifest much about ourselves in the stories we share (often with tedious regularity) with others.

But a sentimental attachment to places of thick time can be dangerous, too, as we've seen in the Middle East, Northern Ireland, Bosnia and elsewhere. Living amid thick time can shackle people to long social memories of past hurts and injustices. Memory dredges up the river bed of the past, bringing to the surface much that would be better left forgotten. Memories can often twist Jesus' command to 'Do this in remembrance of me' to justify violence and cruelty in the name of justice. That is, in fact, the ironic byword for too many places of thick time: doing *this* – bombing, killing, terrorizing, persecuting, oppressing, driving others away – in remembrance of some past hurt or fears. Tribes of memory are the cause of a great deal of misery in our world.

Perhaps then it's better to forget, to embrace the cosmopolitan amnesia that so characterizes our age. Live in the present or, better yet, in the hope of a brighter future. 'Leave the dead to bury the dead' is something else Jesus said that can be repurposed to justify our present impulses. 'Leave the past to bury the past' and embrace the possibilities of the future yet to come. After all, people can enjoy Cadair Idris without knowing the history of the people who have lived within its shadow. Honestly, many of the people who live in the Dysynni Valley probably don't know or care much about its history. The well-to-do commuters and retirees in my former parishes have made those villages more prosperous than anyone before them. Millions of people get by perfectly well without worrying too much about where they work and recreate.

But can we really do that without also losing our souls? Although tribalism is undoubtedly the cause of much mischief, its solution isn't a global culture detached from the land. This is another lesson the earth teaches us. Our global, cosmopolitan society may seem from a narrow perspective to offset any loss of a sense of place with the wealth of goods and services it provides. But how much does that global culture truly cost? How sustainable is a two-dimensional world that neglects its debt to the past and ignores the often distant harm that it causes in the present? I can enjoy my cheap goods, limitless electrical power, supermarkets and petroleum products only because I can't easily see how they're manufactured. I can mindlessly chuck a plastic bottle ring on the ground because I won't see it later strangle a bird to death. I don't mind the loss of community and sense of place because I have a television and a computer to provide me with my own company. If I'm a sensitive soul, I might regret social ills and environmental degradation but probably not as much as I would if my backyard were being toxified, my neighbours exploited, or if I lacked distracting entertainment. In fact, the fantasy world where we enjoy whatever we can afford, develop innovative technologies without any concern for their consequences, and depend on economies that must continually consume comes at an immense and ultimately unsustainable cost to the planet. And ironically, tribalism endures as much as ever, only now it sucks life from ephemeral ideas and ever-changing tastes. We don't call them tribes. We're too sophisticated for that. Instead, we call them identities and lifestyles. Too often, we think of ourselves as belonging to this group or that demographic community rather than to the place where we live and the people who share it with us.

But attachment to place is fundamental to being alive. We're flesh-blood-and-soul individuals dwelling with others in a place, not disembodied minds floating in the ether. Like most creatures we instinctively want to settle, to find our home among our neighbours. Roger Scruton makes this point well:

> The settled person and the nomad differ not only in their experience of space and place, but also in their sense of time. The time of home belongs to . . . the flow that we inwardly experience and which connects past to future through the lived present. . . . To be fully in time, aware of our identity from past to future, we must live according to the regime of responsibility. . . . And time, experienced in that way, connects us to worlds before and after us. The time for which we yearn and to which we gravitate is one that stretches beyond this moment, this person and this life. It is a time in which the dead and the unborn are also present.[3]

To live beyond the moment, we need to settle in places where we can see time manifested around us. The artefacts of the past remind us of

---

[3]Roger Scruton, *Green Philosophy: How to Think Seriously About the Planet* (London: Atlantic Books, 2012), 233–4.

our debt to our forebears and our responsibility to our children. We need tenacious bonds with our parents, grandparents and children to learn the stories that imbue our homes with personality, colour and an enduring social consciousness.

Places of thick time may produce sentimental attachments, but from such connections arise an attitude of care and responsibility that's like the love found in our most familiar relationships. Scruton continues:

> That is why oikophilia [a love for home] leans naturally in the direction of history and the conservation of the past: not from nostalgia, but from a desire to live as an enduring consciousness among things that endure. The true spirit of conservation sees the past not as a commercialized 'heritage', but as a living inheritance, something that lasts because it lives in me. . . . The past lives in us as a place of untaken pathways, of decisions and commitments, and it is by experiencing the world thus that we acquire the sense of stewardship. We come to see that this present moment is also past, but the past of someone else, who has yet to be.[4]

Places of thick time grant us a greater consciousness of time itself, of living within a history that has formed us and from which we've drawn life. We owe our existence not only to our parents but also to the language, customs, ideas, prejudices, joys, stories and relationships that they shared with each other as part of a wider community and imparted to us. Without that culture we would be at best feral and likely mad. One of the crimes of our cosmopolitan culture is to pretend that we owe the past nothing as though each generation sprang fully formed from the ground like Athena from Zeus's head. What the present teaches us is that when we lose our attachment to the past, we invariably lose sight of the future – which will one day be the past for those 'yet to be'.

Wendell Berry argues that forgetting the past also results in our losing respect for the earth. Local memory imparts a sense of responsibility both to the local community and to the landscape in which it's set. Conversely, when we're no longer attached to a specific community and a specific landscape, we usually cease to

---

[4]Ibid., 234–5.

value humanity and the earth in general. 'Those who say, "I love God," and hate their brothers or sisters, are liars; for those who do not love a brother or sister whom they have seen, cannot love God whom they have not seen' (1 John 4.20) – if we don't love what has been given specifically to us, how can we hope to love the things that have been given to humanity generally? Berry warns about the destruction that results:

> It is not easily dismissible that virtually from the beginning of the progress of science-technology-and-industry that we call the Industrial Revolution, while some have been confidently predicting that science, going ahead as it has gone, would solve all problems and answer all questions, others have been in mourning. Among the mourners have been people of the highest intelligence and education, who were speaking, not from nostalgia or reaction or superstitious dread, but from knowledge, hard thought, and the promptings of culture.
>
> What were they afraid of? What were their 'deep-set repugnances'? What did they mourn? Without exception, I think, what they feared, what they found repugnant, was the violation of life by oversimplifying, feelingless utilitarianism; they feared the destruction of the living integrity of creatures, places, communities, cultures, and human souls; they feared the loss of the old prescriptive definition of humankind, according to which we are neither gods nor beasts, though partaking of the nature of both. What they mourned was the progressive death of the earth.5

Places of thick time, therefore, provoke us to adopt a balanced perspective, reminding us that we're just a tiny and ephemeral link in an incredibly long historical chain stretching from time immemorial towards time inconceivable.

-o0o-

Let's return now to my reverie at Castell-y-Bere. Looking north, I could see where the old parish church has stood since the thirteenth

---

5Wendell Berry, *Life Is a Miracle: An Essay against Modern Superstition* (Berkeley: Counterpoint, 2000), 75–6.

century; turning to the west I could admire the valley inhabited by people since the dawn of time and cultivated since before the Romans; the cairns, standing stones and hill forts also speak of enduring ages dimly remembered. In comparison to these ancient monuments I hardly exist. The whole span of my life occupies the most fleeting of moments in the long expanse of human history. I'm no more substantial than a wisp of smoke in comparison to these places.

> [Those] of low estate are but a breath,
>   men of high estate are a delusion;
> in the balances they go up;
>   they are together lighter than a breath. (Ps. 62.9)

The old places will still watch over the Dysynni Valley long after I'm gone and will continue to form part of the imagination of the local residents long after I've been utterly forgotten. The old sites are really only each other's companions, the only permanent residents of the valley and hills. If they were living, just imagine what they would have witnessed. How many great crises and watersheds have they seen come and go? Inhabitants of the hill fort may have thought the world was at an end when the Roman legions arrived to decimate their druids. The defenders of Castell-y-Bere certainly thought all was lost when Edward I's army breached their walls. Parishioners likely bemoaned the dark times when they were told to forsake their old religion after Henry VIII split his Church from Rome. All of these and countless more events have invaded this valley and yet the world continues.

Thick time roots us to a place, allows us to share an identity with others both past and present, and perhaps teaches us a degree of humility. All three protest against our prevailing consumer culture and our conviction that we matter the most. To a society that tries to divorce people from the land by placing them in standardized suburbs with standardized shops, thick time declares, 'The land matters.' To a society that says forget history, forget your neighbours, be whoever you want to be, thick time declares, 'Other people matter.' To a society that says you're free to do anything you want, thick time asks, 'Why be alone when you can belong?' Thick time binds us to others within a historical landscape and disposes us to live beyond ourselves. We're discovering now after so much thick-history has been bulldozed that without it we find it hard to sustain our social fabric and the earth. Only people who have lost their loyalty to their ancestors and to the land can live so as to leave little for their children.

But, of course, thick time actually *does* nothing. Part of its magic lies in the fact that it simply *is* – or perhaps better, it's simply our interaction with what has been and still is within a particular place. I suspect few natives of the Dysynni Valley stop to think about the peculiarity of their place or about how the historical landscape has shaped their sense of self. Many of them probably hardly ever visit the historical sites and are a little mystified that tourists will drive hundreds of miles to visit them. But those places still fill their hearts with a deep affection and a sense of responsibility to that land. It's their home.

It's the nature of a home to take our valuables for granted. Just as we don't stop often enough to appreciate the family rituals, the comfortable furniture, the sounds and smells of the house, and the memories each room contains, so too do we rarely appreciate the interaction between land and time in the location we call home. They simply *are*. Their effect on us is often at the subliminal level and all the more powerful for that. For the subconscious is where our affections meet our imagination and compel our hearts to yield themselves to those places that we sanctify by calling them home.

4

The Incarnation

As I made my way home from Cadair Idris on the following day, I reflected on the juxtaposition of Cwm Cau and the Dysynni Valley. In the one place, time seemed meaningless. It stretched aeons beyond anything I could imagine and was marked only by an unending cycle of seasons and the weather it brought. But, in the other place, time permeated everything. It was inescapable and, from the perspective of my brief experience of it, seemed to define everything in that fertile lowland. Two valleys: in the one I was turned towards the eternal and in the other, towards the historical. I suppose both places shared the quality of drawing me outside of myself. In both places, I found it difficult to be preoccupied with myself even though my personal life was brimming with worries. But the two valleys seemed otherwise juxtaposed, a paradox of landscapes, pulling my thoughts and reflections in opposite directions.

There are few places like Wales where timelessness and thick time dance around each other so intimately. Thoughtful walkers find themselves alternately confronted with both the timeless and the vast expanse of human history. Except where heavy industry and suburban sprawl have wrecked earth and obliterated old landmarks, time and the timeless are locked together in an enduring embrace. Landscapes, villages, buildings, landmarks, stories, place names and customs all come together in a constellation that's rare elsewhere. They convey a history of change amid the changeless like a flash of youth seen on the withered face of an elderly man or woman.

When I used to hike in the Appalachian Mountains, I was often struck by the quality of the changeless. Those ancient mountains have been worn down by the passage of millennia upon millennia and are thickly covered by dense woodlands that feel primordial even if they aren't. Leave the trails and except for the occasional jet plane flying overhead, you can escape all evidence of humanity in those deep woods and find yourself amid utter nature. There are, of course, pockets of thick time in the Appalachians: the old towns with ramshackle buildings, the memories of the largely dispossessed Cherokee often marked now only by place names and the fading local cultures that have resisted the influx of Northern retirees. But my main experience of the Appalachians was of their wilderness where year after year the landscape remained the same even if the details constantly changed – like a waterfall whose shape never alters even though it flows constantly away. I was reminded of this changeless quality a few years ago when I returned to Black Balsam Knob, a favourite spot of mine on the Art Loeb Trail, after a nine-year absence. Much had happened in my own life – emigration to the UK, a PhD earned, five different homes and three jobs, a divorce and a son who had grown into a young man – but when I stood on that spot looking out over the range of blue-green-hued mountains it was as though I'd been there yesterday. Nothing had altered.

In contrast, my regular walking circuits in the Cotswolds often caused me to reflect on the passage of time. I would strap on my daypack and spend the day walking among the prosperous medieval villages and market towns that abound in honey-coloured stone and are cosily set within a long-cultivated landscape. I walked the network of footpaths between Moreton-on-the-March and Winchcombe so often, I could have almost done it blindfolded. You can't escape history in that part of England; if anything, the gentle hills of the Cotswolds convey a sense of thick time even more than the Dysynni Valley with every inch of its earth seemingly worked by centuries of human hands. The old prosperity of the ancient hills and fields there, however, had long ago banished any sense of the ageless. Oxfordshire and the Cotswolds are strikingly lovely, and I'm very fond of their layers of history, but they're not admired for their wild and rugged landscapes. History reigns supreme there even if in a gentrified register.

Wales is different. Here, I've enjoyed walks along trackless moors on uninhabited mountains where I've stumbled upon standing stones keeping vigil as they have done for over four thousand years. Go to Fforest Fawr, a few miles from Brecon where I now live. There you'll find yourself among the sandstone heights of the

Brecon Beacons formed over 360 million years ago and can tromp
(or slog if the weather is wet) across peatland that's been slowly
building up since the glaciers retreated 12,000 years ago. If you like,
you can follow a route that takes you along Sarn Helen, a Roman
road that once crossed the entirety of Wales and now bears the
name of the princess and wife of Macsen Wledig, who came within
an inch of seizing control of the western Roman Empire during the
fourth century. A short detour from there will take you to Maen
Llia, a massive, twelve-feet tall standing sandstone probably erected
during the Bronze Age – thick time and the timeless together again.

Once walking along a wooded road, I stumbled upon an ancient
holy well still gurgling with fresh water and, to my astonishment,
festooned with recent offerings and earnest prayers written on
rain-smeared paper. Just up the slope from there stands a medieval
church, likely marking an even older holy place, in which old wall
paintings gaze towards an altar partially hidden behind an ornately
carved rood screen. That well found in the old, mossy wooded
slopes of the Black Mountains may have been a holy site since long
before the first Christian missionaries reached this benighted corner
of the crumbling Roman Empire. Time embraces the timeless again.
Elsewhere, I once followed an otherwise ordinary path that took
me past a massive outcropping into which pilgrims of old roughly
carved a cross to mark their passage. Wales abounds in timeless
landscapes where one can find reminders of long-forgotten human
habitation.

I think the hill forts are what most capture my imagination. Some
of them are in incredibly remote places, now sheltering sodden
sheep instead of valiant warriors. Most of them are nothing to look
at anymore and have long since been robbed of anything that might
tell archaeologists much about their history. But enough has been
excavated for us to know that some of these sites were occupied
for hundreds of years. That simply astounds me. These barren sites
gradually melting back into rock and turf were once inhabited
far longer than the United States has existed. Some mark over a
thousand years of history now forever forgotten. Think of the lives
lived, the loves shared, the hopes expressed, the gods worshipped,
the stories retold and the deaths mourned that now leave no trace
whatsoever. Those places once housed long-enduring communities
rich in memory, customs and politics that now have totally and
irrevocably vanished. Stand in a hill fort pondering its long- and

forever-forgotten history and you quickly realize how ephemeral so much of civilization is. In places like Pen-y-crug, Twyn y Gaer and Crug Hywel, hill forts near where I now live, thick time has long ago been swallowed up by the timelessness of the landscape.

In such sites, I'm reminded that in Wales thick time and timelessness don't really compete as you might expect. In almost every instance they seem suited to each other like an elderly couple in the twilight of a long marriage – the timeless frames thick time and thick time seems most at home within timeless landscapes. Both provide the unchanging frontier to the manic, ever-changing flow of human activity. The mountains and deep valleys long knew a world in which there were no *homo sapiens* seeking new ways to exploit them for minerals and shelter. But they've also seen a long procession of peoples arriving, thriving and vanishing. How many people living among them now stop to think of the Neolithic, Celtic, Roman, medieval and early modern people who knew those same hills? To the hills and mountains, all human activity is like a brief flash or an ever-changing cloud of smoke. In comparison to them, among us there's no permanence, no sitting still.

The closest we've come to permanence are the ancient ruins, stone circles, place names, field systems and age-worn churches sheltered in that landscape. These monuments are tangible evidence of our long acquaintance with these timeless places. They're also our only solidity. Their age is their entry pass onto the threshold of the timeless that permits them to share with the hills and mountains the privilege of enduring while everything else appears, vanishes, and is soon forgotten. But they can never go further than the threshold – ruins crumble to dust, names are forgotten and even ancient churches are turned to other uses and are gutted. 'All flesh is like grass and all its glory like the flower of grass. The grass withers, and the flower falls' (1 Pet. 1.24) – words often uttered at funerals. We like to think of ourselves as mighty builders and ingenious devisers of enduring laws, customs and civilizations. The timeless mountains and the crumbling ruins of long-forgotten builders laugh us to scorn.

Yet, like the landscapes in which they're set, these relics have seen generations of people busy with their daily concerns. Take as an example Garth Hill near where I once lived outside of Cardiff in South Wales. At least once a week, I would take Cuthbert for a walk up a steep path cut through deep bracken to the top of the hill. From atop an overhanging rock, I could look down on a valley of change: old, terraced homes built for mining families and new estates for commuters jostle for space against massive warehouses and industrial plants. Through the heart of these restless communities flows a constant stream of traffic emitting a relentless and inescapable din. It's like looking down at a disturbed anthill, with everything frantically chasing around and nothing seeming to stand still. Progress and modernity are pronounced by the place's very design, which runs like an ugly scar up the long valley where industry has dominated since the Napoleonic Wars.

But when I continued along the top of the Garth and away from that view – typically in driving rain or a gathering evening fog – I encountered another world. Bronze Age burial mounds covered by the dense turf mark the broad crest of the hill. They've been there since time immemorial and are now as much a part of the high hill as the outcropping of rock or the dense carpet of bracken. Like the Garth, those burial mounds have gazed down upon Iron Age Silures, prosperous Romans, invading Saxons, Marcher Lords, reforming Protestants and greedy industrialists, and they've watched nearby Cardiff grow from nothing into the sprawling capitol it is today. In that respect, those mounds are like the hill upon which they were built. In comparison to us, they *do* enjoy solidity, and in their permanence have become companions to the timeless hill. Those who live and have grown up in the shadow of the Garth would be outraged if they awoke one morning to find the burial mounds flattened.

The same contrast between permanence and the ephemeral can be found in countless places in Wales: the monuments of thick-history and the changelessness of the landscape belong to each other and are apart from us. They share the honour of permanence and endurance that we've not earned and, therefore, like our elders deserve our respect and perhaps even our deference. We should feel a reverence for them and protect them from our insatiable appetite to tinker because these sentinels are vital reminders that we live within a natural and historical environment too ancient for us to even begin to conceive. They remind us of our own impermanence and, thus too, of the frailty of our endeavours. Stand among the foundations of an ancient hut village on Anglesey or the crumbling stone of Dolwyddelan Castle or the remnants of Valle Crucis Abbey and you'll find it hard to be deceived by the illusion that our own achievements are necessarily any more enduring than they.

We do reverence these places. Their continued existence proves that. Even in an age when we dig up and tear down at a frenetic pace, we know without really having to be told that these sites are special. Yes, hooligans may vandalize them, but this is almost always met with an outrage altogether different from the anger we feel when a shop, bridge or even modern piece of art is defaced. We know in our gut that these ancient sites are important and that we are responsible for them, even if we can't quite articulate that duty. And we recognize this quality about even distant ancient places as seen by the worldwide outrage over the destruction of Syrian sites by ISIS. In their destruction, the loss of such places – only pinpointed on a map of the globe – impoverishes everyone.

Yet, I don't think we reverence these places in the same way as we once did. Now, we tend to 'manage' timeless landscapes and ancient monuments. We must or else rapacious developers will readily build houses or a mall or anything else that can turn a profit. But I think we need to think carefully about land and site management, otherwise something of their detachment from us is lost even though their natural resources and beauty may be preserved. The same is even more true of our antiquities: reconstructing and drastically refurbishing ancient monuments or bottling history in 'living museums' risks dispelling their participation in thick-history. Those sites are turned into fabricated snapshots of a past made subject to the preoccupations of the present. As David Lowenthal argues in the introduction to his *The Heritage Crusade and the Spoils of History*, 'heritage is not an inquiry into past but a celebration of it, not an effort to know what actually happened but a profession of faith in a past tailored to present-day purposes'.[1]

Obviously, this has to an extent always been the case, usually at the behest of those in power to bolster their own ideology. Today, heritage tends to be the preserve of academics, experts, managers and marketers who determine their identities. That's why I avoid a great many popular historical sites – they're often infuriatingly didactic as though the only reason for their preservation is to teach swarms of largely bored schoolchildren about what it was like to live in the past (often with the implicit message that they

---

[1]David Lowenthal, *The Heritage Crusade and the Spoils of History* (Cambridge: Cambridge University Press, 1997), x.

should be more grateful for what they enjoy in the present). Too many historical places have really been turned into tributes to the supposedly enlightened present, disposing people to celebrate the wonders that social and technological progress have given us.

Again, I'm realistic enough to understand that such management and even the intrusion of business enterprise may be our only recourse with many important sites. But we should mourn the loss of their authentic life when we're forced to 'manage' an environment that otherwise would do well without us. My own view is that many historic sites should continue to be used or else protected from development as they're allowed to fall into ruin. The alternative, too, often makes our historical places tourist attractions that separate them from the stream of local history. In fact, developing historical sites for tourism is largely a modern phenomenon: a result, I suspect, of the ever-widening fissure between us and our past that characterizes consumer culture. Only when the past becomes utterly foreign, do people begin to visit its relics more for entertainment than out of reverence – it's almost too typical of us to debase 'heritage' into an industry.

The role of management is a little trickier when it comes to the wilderness and the countryside. As wild and timeless as some of these places may seem, most of them are the product of human interaction, even if that's nothing more than the designation of an area as off-limits to development. Moreover, how we conceive of the wilderness – the very fact that we think of them as *wilderness* – is itself a cultural artefact. The environmental historian Bill Cronon writes:

> The more one knows of its peculiar history, the more one realizes that wilderness is not quite what it seems. Far from being the one place on earth that stands apart from humanity, it is quite profoundly a human creation – indeed, the creation of very particular human cultures at very particular moments in human history. It is not a pristine sanctuary where the last remnant of an untouched, endangered, but still transcendent nature can for at least a little while longer be encountered without the contaminating taint of civilization. Instead, it's a product of that civilization, and could hardly be contaminated by the very stuff of which it is made. Wilderness hides its unnaturalness behind a mask that is all the more beguiling because it seems so natural.

As we gaze into the mirror it holds up for us, we too easily imagine that what we behold is Nature when in fact we see the reflection of our own unexamined longings and desires.[2]

Yet, the loss of wild places is now beginning to be felt strongly enough in places like Britain for some to campaign for rewilding. Of course, even such rewilding is a form of management just as American wildernesses often require the careful care of the government in order to remain wild.

There's a difference, though, between the organic laying down of meaning onto landscapes by the people who live within them and the assigning of meaning by experts from elsewhere. One of the problems with rational management is that it brings our landscapes and historical sites under the control of experts. To put this another way: it lashes the enduring to the transient. The relationship between a community and its landscape and history is vital for stability and a sense of place. The combination of the timeless and thick-history of a landscape exerts its influence on the people who live there for generations. In turn, those people, often without even thinking about it, express their relationship to that landscape through the stories they create and share. We'll talk more about this later, but among the most powerful forces in the world are shared stories rooted in shared landscapes. Those stories give definition to our sense of faithfulness, compelling us to measure other stories by how well they fit with our sense of belonging in *this* place and among *these* people.

Once those places become intrusively managed, however, two things happen. First, all too often outside experts are brought in to explain why the site is being conserved. In effect, people are told what to think about the place. If it's a nature reserve, they're informed that it needs to be placed off-limits and managed in order to protect wildlife or a particular kind of environment (like wetlands). Such conservation is, of course, vital and I applaud the efforts of people to ensure such places continue to exist and thrive. But again, once that happens, the relationship of the communities in the area to that landscape changes, especially if a car park and

---

[2]Bill Cronon, *Uncommon Ground: Rethinking the Human Place in Nature* (New York: W.W. Norton & Company, 1996), 1.

facilities are built to attract nature lovers from elsewhere. If it's a historic site, then informative signs, visitor centres, guidebooks and the like wrestle control from the stories and local lore that site may have produced within the local community. Local memory yields to official expertise and outside planning. We value the accurate facts of experts more highly than the enduring (though often inaccurate) local lore that has been sufficiently engaging to endure from generation to generation. When this happens, local sites no longer really belong to their community since even locals can now gain entry only in the same way as visitors from the most distant places: by paying an entry fee. In effect, by making them attractions, such places are dis-embedded from their social and cultural environment except insofar as they can generate income by attracting tourists.

Second, managed landscapes become subject to economic forces and, like everything else, must therefore be justified financially and marketed to attract custom. Management is an expensive business and can't long be sustained without the cash of crowds of visitors. So, people are encouraged to vacation in places of natural beauty. Yosemite is a prime example: it may be preserved for posterity, but the fleets of campers and the hordes of outdoor enthusiasts (over four million per year) have turned it into something altogether different from a proper wilderness. Historic sites put on concerts and other major events to draw people from far and wide to support the costs of preserving such places (or they're promoted as potential film locations). In effect, such places are commodified, turned into businesses, and thus are stripped from the local community to whose history they really belong. In Britain, the heritage industry brings in more than £10 billion, more than agriculture and aerospace combined. The countryside and our historic places have become the preserve of the tourist industry.

In his *The Shepherd's Life: A Tale of the Lake District*, James Rebanks recounts how it can feel for locals to discover they live in a place managed and defined by others. His first experience of being an outsider in his own home was in school where he was taught about the Lake District as though the people who lived and worked there didn't matter. He recalls:

> After a few minutes of listening, I realised this bloody teacher woman thought we were too stupid and unimaginative to 'do anything with our lives'. . . . We were too dumb to want to leave

the area with its dirty dead-end jobs and its narrow-minded provincial ways.

For her, the Lake District wasn't home to enduring agricultural communities, but the 'playground for an itinerant band of climbers, poets, walkers and daydreamers'.[3]
Later, Rebanks even bemoans the hugely popular Wainwright walking guides – little short of bibles for walkers besotted with the Lakes – for creating a perception of the Lake District in which Rebanks's own people hardly appear:

> Apart from the odd dot on the map for a farm or a wall, nothing from our world appeared in those pages. I wonder whether the people on the mountain saw the working side of that landscape, and whether it mattered. In my bones I felt it did matter. That seeing, understanding and respecting people in their own landscapes is crucial to their culture and ways of life being valued and sustained. What you don't see, you don't care about.[4]

After more than a hundred years of government policies and planning, the Lake District exists more in the national imagination as a middle-class 'playground' than it does in the lived experience and heritage of the people who have lived and worked its rich lands and called it home. Places like the Lake District can now be multiplied thousands of times over.
I admit that I'm being unfair here. We normally have no other choice but to preserve such places through tourism since we've manifestly proven ourselves otherwise incapable of honouring and respecting them. Beatrix Potter didn't fight to conserve the Lakes for them to become a managed playground but in order to prevent them being destroyed by encroaching development. Besides, consumer culture has created a deep fissure between us and our past that undermines relationships to local heritage except as tourist attractions. If you relentlessly tell people that the past should be discarded and the future embraced, don't be surprised if they do precisely that. Instead, the only social language of value we know is

[3]James Rebanks, *The Shepherd's Life: A Tale of the Lake District* (London: Penguin, 2015), xiv–xv.
[4]Ibid., 88.

that of commerce, and so historical and natural places must prove themselves useful for them to be valued.

I think parish churches in the UK illustrate this point: for many people, they no longer are real sources of meaning in their lives, except nostalgically or as aesthetic backdrops for key moments of life: birth, marriage and death. Most parish churches can no longer sustain themselves organically through the love and care of the communities that worship in them and so must explore creative finance. The collapse of their regular use by local communities during the past sixty years is due as much to our separation from our own past as to our loss of faith (I suspect the two are intricately intertwined). The world in which they provided social meaning and cohesion is now almost as foreign as the one that built hill forts.

Thus, the work done by conservationists, nonprofits and preservation societies is invaluable, and I'm thankful for all they do. My issue has more to do with the society that demands their existence. That world to my mind is defined by two impulses: the first is to bring everything under our control to serve the interests of national industry, and the second is to detach itself from history. According to the first impulse, spaces should be either developed or preserved for profit. What can't be tolerated easily is for space to be left *without a function*, even if that function is nothing more than to provide a green space for the well-being of people with leisure time. According to the second impulse, local histories are discarded in favour of the cosmopolitan – tradition must yield to progress and innovation. The cold fact of the matter is that a field is just a field even if long ago for a day it was the site of a terrible battle. If now it's only an expanse of grass in a prime location, then why not build a shopping mall on it or a Disney historical theme park as was once proposed for part of the Manassas National Battlefield Park in Virginia?

Consequently, people become disconnected from the thick-history that shaped their local communities for generations; the places that produce thick-history are gelded and so are impotent to influence either our present or future. The second impulse would see the destruction of a great many landscapes while the first preserves them only as commodities of consumption. The result is a vastly different relationship with history and our timeless spaces than at any other period. Our nature reserves and castles are more like shopping malls and theme parks than we probably care to admit.

-o0o-

Timelessness and thick time need each other and we, them. That's what my experience of the Dysynni Valley and Cwm Cau taught me. Certainly, both places are to a degree managed. Cadair Idris has a car park, visitor's centre and shop and is ringed by campgrounds. It draws walkers from across the UK and abroad and regularly hosts fitness challenges and charity events. In the early hours of the morning, I was startled from my sleep by a band of climbers presumably completing the Welsh 3000s Challenge, during which men and women attempt to climb all the Welsh mountains over 3,000 feet in one go. I watched their head torches bob like will o' the wisps up the precipitous slope in the blackness of that moonless night before settling back into my sleeping bag. Cadair Idris is far from being an unspoilt wilderness.

Fortunately for the valley, the castle draws comparatively few visitors and remains free of charge for any to enter. That landscape is a husbanded one, mostly shaped by the local farmers who care for the place they call home. In an interview for S4C, one local farmer expressed this very sentiment when he described himself and his fellow farmers as 'wardens as long as we live here'. Their allegiance isn't to a vast industry, a distant bureaucracy or tourism; rather, it's to their parents and grandparents and to their children and grandchildren. Ultimately, too, their loyalty is to the landscape that they call home.

Both Cwm Cau and the Dysynni Valley caused me to reflect on the paradoxical relationship between history and timelessness, eternity and time. That they should impress on me a deep sense of togetherness is strange. Cultures and religions have tended to keep them far apart. Eternity is where the divine dwells, accessible only to the soul, if at all. Time is limited to our world, this place of changeable human beings, changeable creatures and changeable weather. And between the two lies an unbridgeable chasm: the one place transcends any human influence while the other is the arena for all human activity. 'Eternity and time: two entirely separate things,' Plotinus wrote in his *Enneads*.[5] Philosophers and theologians have described these two spheres as the transcendent and the imminent, but they've gone by other names as well: superlunary and sublunary, supernatural and natural, heaven and earth. And the chasm that separates these two realms has only widened since the Enlightenment so that God seems so very distant and his reach into this world – our world –

---

[5]Plotinus, *Enneads*, trans. Stephen MacKenna (London: Penguin, 1991), 45.1.

so very tenuous. This world is definite, observable, measurable, quantifiable, *real*; God's world is only subjective, shadowy, imagined and, ultimately (some believe and many fear), a fantasy.

But then we find within the Christian tradition the strange belief that time and eternity are meant for one another: 'For us and for our salvation, he came down from heaven: by the power of the Holy Spirit he became incarnate from the Virgin Mary, and was made man.' God became man; Eternity wrapped himself in time; the Changeless grew from a fertilized egg to a middle-aged man before dying cruelly on a rough-hewn cross. In the person of Jesus Christ, early theologians recognized not only that the divine 'became flesh and lived among us' but also that eternity's piercing into time revealed how thin the veil that divides heaven and earth actually is.

In the Old Testament, God's realm and our world were seen as lying far apart except in the confined space of the Ark of Covenant and later the Holy of Holies where heaven and earth intersected. God could reveal himself in our world – they called this *glory* – but except for the fire and cloud of Exodus this almost invariably came as a voice or through angelic intermediaries. God's appearances in this world were only brief and intangible encounters. He couldn't be seen or touched, let alone embraced. In that sense, his sporadic appearances served to accentuate his usual absence, not least during those many times when Israel suffered. 'Why, O Lord, do you stand far off? / Why do you hide yourself in times of trouble?' (Ps. 10.1) speaks to the common experience of humanity's relationship with God.

The Greek response to this situation was to develop a philosophical means for some people to climb a mystical ladder away from this world to the divine. Discipline the mind through study, virtue and bodily self-control, devote yourself to contemplating the divine, and don't become distracted by the changeable things of this world, and your soul will be properly prepared at your death to escape the prison of earthly life to return to the Elysium of divine union. Oh, and by the way, make sure you're male and wealthy enough to afford the leisure for study and contemplation. In other words, the path to the divine lay only through abandoning this world totally: the divine and this world were imagined as not only distant but also opposed. This remains the bias of many Eastern religions.

'God became flesh and lived among us' is therefore one of the most radical religious claims ever made. The Prologue to John's Gospel doesn't insist on our ascending to a distant God. Rather, it asserts unabashedly that God entered into the theatre of our own existence, took on our flesh and blood, and set his feet firmly on the dusty soil of first-century Palestine. Jesus explicitly claimed to be the one in whom heaven and earth meet: he pronounced the divine forgiveness of sins (which could happen only in the Temple) and he declared that he would tear down the Temple and rebuild it in three days. The allusion to his own Resurrection as a rebuilding of the Temple shows that Easter represents not only the forgiveness of sins and the conquest of death but also the nuptial union of heaven and earth, of eternity and time.

Working out the theological ramifications of the Incarnation led to one of the greatest intellectual revolutions of the ancient world: namely, the acknowledgement that *this world* matters. In much of Greek and Near Eastern thought, this world is merely an illusion, a distraction from all that's immutable and eternal. Plato, for example, imagined our world – the place of fomenting fire, air, water and earth – to be only a 'moving image' of the eternal: real enough to those within it but actually tottering on the brink of nothingness like shadows on a wall. This world exists as a place from which the imprisoned souls of wise and pure men must try to escape by dedicating themselves to the contemplation of the divine.

The Incarnation, however, required Christians to accept that this world does matter, that God believes that this world is worth his dwelling in and dying for. This point is emphasized even more by his Resurrection: that Christ rose from the dead and ascended to heaven in bodily form rather than as a spirit demonstrates that in his plan of redemption, God doesn't intend to cast away this world as so much rubbish. This belief was ridiculous to the Greeks that St Paul encountered in his missionary journeys, and he saw it as evidence that God used folly to shame the wise and save those who believe (1 Cor. 1.20-31). Indeed, the great vision of the heavenly Jerusalem that concludes the New Testament presents the eternal descending in the form of city into this ravaged world: the very opposite of our own assumptions that time must somehow be swallowed up in eternity. That vision implies, I think, that God becoming man wasn't a one-off event but a pattern for redeemed life: the eternal dwelling in the historical and the changeless inhabiting the ephemeral. Perhaps the fullness of God in the form of an infant lying in a manger isn't something to be thought of only at Christmas but is the shape of our Christian hope. Hard to wrap our minds around? Certainly. Nonsensical? You bet. But that's the nature of a paradox, isn't it?

At the same time, for us truly to stand open to the eternal, I'm convinced that we must plant our feet firmly in the historical. God wants his holy people *earthed*. The quality of thick time is to make us receptive to the timeless because it draws our imaginations away from the here and now and helps us to keep a tight rein on that fantasy we call the future. Christ the eternal Word became enfleshed not as a generic human being (whatever that is) but as a Jew whose identity owed everything to the thick time encoded in his identity through their traditions and customs. The Jewishness of Jesus is as important as his divinity. Yes, Jesus became man and dwelt among us, but the man he became was thoroughly Jewish as the church recalls, for example, on 1 January and 2 February when we celebrate his circumcision and presentation at the Temple, respectively. In other words, the reason why God became man only really made sense to those like St Paul who were planted firmly within the long history of Israel, which had taught them how to recognize the eternal.

Christianity today seems intent on detaching itself from its own thick time. We don't teach our children the Bible or about the saints, few religious education programmes emphasize church history anymore and our worship seems increasingly to embrace the novel and to abandon anything deemed old-fashioned. We've lost sense of the thick-history of Christianity that has formed individuals and societies across cultures and time. We risk not only succumbing to ecclesial amnesia but also inuring ourselves to the eternal, leaving us only with the ephemeral – the never-ending procession of fashions and fancies that so afflict the church. Whenever Israel forgot her own past, she invariably forsook God for the worship of idols; similarly, if we forget our Christian past, we'll continue to chase after the idols of our own age: self-expression, self-affirmation and self-identity.

Instead, we need to enable people to be receptive to the eternal by rooting them in the deep currents of time. Only in that way can we begin to plumb the depths of what it means for God to have become man, for heaven to have entered this world, for eternity to have pierced to the very marrow of our existence. In the palm of eternity all time has been redeemed, not by being overwhelmed or swallowed up, but by containing the uncontainable like the Ark once contained God's glory and the Virgin, her Lord.

PART II

The paradox of silence and words

FIGURE 2 *An early morning view down at Llyn Cau.*

Trinity! Higher than any being, any divinity, and goodness!
Guide of Christians in the wisdom of heaven! Lead us up beyond
unknowing and light, up to the farthest, highest peak of mystic
scripture, where the mysteries of God's Word lie simple, absolute
and unchangeable in the brilliant darkness of a hidden silence.
PSEUDO-DIONYSIUS, Mystical Theology

5

Craig Lwyd

Silence

After I finished my pint of ale, I prepared a spicy dinner of Thai noodles in my old JetBoil. Then a minor disaster struck. I turned my attention away just long enough for a devilish gust of wind to blow the boiler over, spilling the half-cooked noodles amid a large scattering of sheep droppings. Thus, my reflections on eternity and time ended in a prosaic tragedy marked by a loud groan and a few curses as my dinner seeped into the earth, leaving an unedifying glop of egg noodles and sheep shit. I had to settle for a handful of cashews and a chocolate bar for my meagre dinner – hardly ideal after lugging a backpack all day in the mountains.

Still, it takes more than the loss of a £2 pack of noodles to spoil my mood. So, with sunset approaching, I decided to climb to the top of Craig Lwyd, on the south side of Cadair Idris, to enjoy the view of the high hills of southern Snowdonia as the sky slowly faded from a rich gold to the lapis lazuli of the evening. Fifteen hundred feet below me spread a deep valley in which lay the long, dark form of Tal-y-llyn, the lake from which the river Dysynni flows into the Irish Sea. The lights of Ty'n y Cornel Hotel glowed brilliantly in the gathering gloom, reflecting dimly off the still waters of the lake. Across from me, the long mountain of Graig Goch loomed like a shadowy wall over the valley; invisible now in the darkening dusk were the features of its steep slopes carved out by a prehistoric landslide that dammed up the lake below. Soon the stars would be out, and I would carefully make my way back down to my tent by the light of my head torch. For now, though, I hunkered down as comfortably as I could amid a rocky outcrop scattered there during the violence of a volcano 500 million years ago.

Perched as I was nearly 2,000 feet above sea level and away from any human habitation, I should have been able to enjoy some peace. But even from that great height, the din of modernity made itself heard: the constant hum of cars barrelling along the A487. In the deepening shadows of the mountains, their headlights reminded me of sparks flying along a circuit – artful in their own way but also incongruous in that otherwise peaceful and dark environment. It struck me how bizarre it was that such miniscule lights – smaller than fireflies from my height – could produce such noise. The automobile is a singularly loud contraption. I considered the passengers of those cars with their radios blaring, oblivious to the silent world their brief incursion was shattering. Our cars are capsules of noise transporting us through an otherwise quiet world.

After about an hour of sitting atop Craig Lwyd in happy reverie, my back had had enough of the sharp-edged rock that was my backrest, and I was ready for a hot cup of tea. So, I carefully picked my way back down the path to my tent by the light of my head torch. My descent back down the stony path was also a descent into a deep silence harboured within the havening heights around Cwm Cau. Having ruined my dinner, the wind had moved on to trouble others, leaving in its wake a silence that was only broken by sheep calling out 'yeah' to each other and the faint crunch of their relentless munching of grass and heather. I was utterly alone in the dark of that high valley with just the faintest light of the moon and stars to pick out one feature from another. Hot cup of tea in hand, I was enshrouded by the kind of silence you only experience away from human habitation and in the darkness of a wilderness.

Nothing compares to the silence of nature. It's nothing like a sound-proofed room or sound-cancelling earphones, for it has the quality of magnitude. You can feel the space around you in a way you can't in daylight. You can almost hear – or at least want to hear – the music of the spheres because the silence seems to stretch to the stars themselves. Indeed, at moments like that I begin to wonder if the ancient cosmologists didn't have it right after all – at least, the planets and stars seem much nearer and more companionable than how they're described in our textbooks. In our scientific enlightenment, we may know them to be millions of miles away, but when I lay against a cold rock gazing up at them, it seemed to me that they belonged entirely to the landscape. Were it not for the glimmer of stars and the bright shine of the moon gradually creeping up over the shadowy cliffs, all would lie in darkness. It was by their dim light that I could discern the dark landscape around me.

And the silence I was then enjoying really did stretch to the stars. If I'd somehow ascended from Cwm Cau into outer space, I would have risen through varying degrees of silence until I reached the absolute silence of outer space. Ridley Scott's sci-fi horror film *Alien* carried the chilling tagline, 'In space, no one can hear you scream.' That's because ours is a silent cosmos, which apparently the creators of almost every sci-fi film don't understand. No growling TIE fighters or whooping starships accelerating to WARP speed. Just the infinite quiet of dark space. In that sense, our planet is not unlike the cars that had ruined my quiet reverie: a capsule of noise in an otherwise soundless cosmos.

The indescribable vastness of the world's silence was the third element of my happy evening on Cadair Idris. It was an essential element, too, for without it I would never have fallen into the reflective mood that made me aware of the intimate dance of timelessness and thick time. Like the other two elements, the most powerful effect of the vast quiet was to make me feel inconsequential. Now, that may sound dreadful to you. But for me, it was freeing. In the grand scheme of things, I don't matter. Were I to vanish now, the mountains, the old castle, Mary Jones's ancient chapel, the sheep, ravens and the distant stars wouldn't care at all. They would be no more affected by my passing than by each autumn's leaf-fall.

I find that thought liberating.

Only a month before his succumbing to cancer, the great neurologist and author, Oliver Sacks, poignantly described a similar sentiment evoked by the silent stars:

> A few weeks ago, in the country, far from the lights of the city, I saw the entire sky 'powdered with stars' (in Milton's words); such a sky, I imagined, could be seen only on high, dry plateaus like that of Atacama in Chile (where some of the world's most powerful telescopes are). It was this celestial splendor that suddenly made me realize how little time, how little life, I had

left. My sense of the heavens' beauty, of eternity, was inseparably mixed for me with a sense of transience – and death.[1]

That experience of the 'night sky full of stars' struck him more powerfully than all the letters of love and support he'd received. While he never explains why that was so, he subsequently began to fill his life with what he called 'emblems of eternity': rocks and minerals free from both life and death. Yet, in his column one also detects a healthy resignation to death, an acceptance that it must come, can't be avoided, that it cares not a jot if we rail against it. In the silence of the starry night, he found a degree of inner peace.

Sacks's experience is a fine example of the effect of silence on us: it gives voice to our innermost selves. Starved of sound and interaction, we find it hard to resist encountering ourselves in the silence of our souls. We're confronted by our fears, hopes, memories both happy and sad, the feelings that are lurking beneath our outward façade and that mysterious voice we know well, which seems other than us and yet is us, who speaks to us, and can be a friend or enemy, a truth-teller, or a deceiver. So much lurks in the quiet of our inner selves: depths upon depths to be plumbed if only we escape the noisy commotions of the external world.

The wanderer and conservationist John Muir famously wrote, 'I only went out for a walk and finally concluded to stay out till sundown, for going out, I found, was really going in.'[2] The deliberate act of leaving behind the everyday and entering into the quiet of nature draws us into ourselves. Perhaps it's our need for companionship that causes us to turn, in solitude, to the only possible partner – our own souls – and to dwell for a time in conversation and familiarity with that stranger who is our very self. When going out from the distractions of this world we can't help but go into ourselves, to re-enter those forgotten and neglected chambers of our psyche.

In my experience, Muir's going out in order to go in usually happens in two phases. The first is the more difficult: starved of distractions the inner voice erupts with chatter as the mind whirrs

[1]Oliver Sacks, 'My Periodic Table', New York Times, 24 July 2015.
[2]Linnie M. Wolfe, John of the Mountains: The Unpublished Journals of John Muir (Madison: University of Wisconsin Press, 2009), 427.

with the din of pressing thoughts. Barely submerged anxieties can suddenly pop up from beneath the surface of our superficial reflections like a thousand buoys of ill-feeling. People prone to overthinking and self-criticism find this period especially tough to endure and to escape – it's the bane of would-be contemplatives and meditators. Here, silence is paradoxically noisy: our incessant, prattling inner voice won't be quiet and we become acutely conscious of time. A ravishing landscape helps: its beauty has a way of drawing us out of ourselves and into herself. Her charms are hard to resist for long. The habit of hiking also helps. When I first began walking regularly, I found the period of active thought stretched out for what seemed like ages, but now I weather it like passing rain and quickly find myself in the more peaceful, contemplative phase.

The second phase of going in by going out is delightful. The mind at long last stills, time elasticates and you increasingly dwell in your surroundings. The inner quiet that settles the soul isn't absolute. The mind still speaks but the thoughts come slowly, and the inner monologue settles into soft background noise or becomes like drowsy conversation. Like slipping into the twilit regions of sleep, time changes and in a strange but comforting way becomes somehow disconnected from you as an individual. There's a freedom in this. This is because your mind is now elsewhere, not in an Age of Aquarius sort of way, but simply because you've been drawn into the quiet that resides beneath your thoughts and feelings. If you're like me, you won't even be conscious of this – the thoughts remain and have your attention, but their intervals elongate so that you dwell increasingly and unconsciously in the timeless moments in between them. It is, I suppose, a kind of extended daydreaming.

This is the magic of prolonged silence: it gives voice to our innermost selves. Starved of sound and interaction, we find it hard to resist encountering ourselves in the stillness of our souls. So much lurks in the silence of our inner selves. In the words of poet-priest Thomas Traherne: 'the soul is a miraculous abyss of infinite abysses, and undrainable ocean, an inexhausted fountain of endless oceans.'[3] We have but to escape the commotion of the external world to discover it.

---

[3]Thomas Traherne, *Centuries* (New York: Harper & Brothers, 1960), II.83.

A few years ago, I decided (almost on a whim) to go trekking for a few days by myself in the Sunnmøre Alps in Norway. I'd never done anything like it before. I flew from Cardiff to Ålesund, a fetching Art Nouveau city nestled among an archipelago of craggy isles that hug dark-watered fjords. The next morning, I caught a bus and a ferry to Sykkylven and walked southward to the trailhead at the top of Brunstaddalen, a narrow valley that pierces into the alpine range. For three days, I hiked alone in a foreign landscape amid the snow-covered rock of those sharp, majestic mountains. I was there early for the season (in fact, I had to alter my route because the snow had yet to melt in the mountain passes) and so encountered not a soul during those three days. It was an eerily quiet landscape, its tranquillity punctuated on the first day only by the magical sound of bells dangling from the necks of scattered sheep and the deep rumble of small avalanches spilling down the steep face of the mountains.

That silence, however, drew me into itself and quieted my mind. It seemed like my inner voice never shut up, not least on the second day when I realized the snow-trapped passes were forcing me to make an eight-mile detour with no obvious camping sites marked on my map. Eventually, I found a flat spot in a closed-for-the-season ski resort high above the Geirangerfjord, pitched my tent and sat with my dinner and a hot drink admiring the tableaux of white-capped mountains, green valleys and the blue waters of the narrow fjord. As I reflected on my trek, I realized that all my thoughts during the two days of walking didn't amount to the actual time spent by myself in the Norwegian wilderness. Someone once said that music is the silence between the notes; similarly, we're the mysterious and too-neglected silence between our thoughts. That silence should remind us that we exist beyond and beneath those thoughts.

Perhaps this was the important insight of Platonists. Their belief that wisdom is acquired by the soul ascending towards the divine was a recognition of our need to be quiet, to withdraw from the busy world around us and simply to dwell within ourselves for a time. Their mystical ascent began with the would-be philosopher retreating inwardly in order to encounter the transcendent. As he dived ever deeper into his own soul, he paradoxically also rose higher into the ethereal cosmos towards the divine. This is what they called contemplation and it required a silence that went beyond the mere lack of noise towards something much more profound, primordial and eternal. In Plotinus's *Enneads*, nature tells the reader not to ask questions but 'learn in silence just as I am silent'.[4] Elsewhere, Plotinus gives this silence another name: existence. The rather pat modern way of expressing this might be to say that we go from *doing* to *being*.

I must confess that though I've spent much of my academic life studying the works of Neoplatonists, I've always had little patience for their pessimistic view of nature and physicality. But they got contemplation right. We need the time and opportunity to enter our own souls in order to encounter God and ourselves. This is what the author Martin Laird calls entering 'into the silent land', where we can reflect on our experiences and strive to gain some perspective on this massive morass of sensory data we call reality.[5] Above all, it's where we encounter God. Laird writes, 'Silence is an urgent necessity for us; silence is necessary if we are to hear God speak in eternal silence; our own silence is necessary if God is to hear us.'[6]

A classical way of imagining this inward movement is as a withdrawal into an inner chamber. We see this, for example, at the start of St Anselm's little meditation *Proslogion*:

> Come now, insignificant man, fly for a moment from your affairs, escape for a little while from the tumult of your thoughts. Put aside now your weighty care and leave your wearisome toils. Abandon yourself for a little to God and rest for a little in Him. Enter into the inner chamber of your soul, shut out everything save God and what can be of help in your quest for Him and having locked the door seek Him out.[7]

That description, not to mention his subsequent ascent towards God that culminates in delight, illustrates the silent movement into our inner selves that is Christian contemplation. The great mystics do this by sitting quietly in their own cells. I need the theatre of nature to achieve the same – but my experience in the Sunnmøre

---

[4]Plotinus, *Enneads*, 3.8.4.
[5]Martin Laird, *Into the Silent Land: A Guide to the Christian Practice of Contemplation* (New York: Oxford University Press, 2006), 3.
[6]Ibid., 2.
[7]Anselm of Canterbury, *Proslogion* in *The Major Works*, ed. Brian Davies and G. R. Evans (Oxford: Oxford University Press, 1998), I.

Alps (and many similar ones elsewhere) has taught me what such contemplation *feels* like and the good it does for my mind, spirit and soul.

When I try to explain this feeling to others, I invariably think of water. Our normal lives are like swimming just beneath the surface. The water makes us a little panicky because we can't breathe, uncomfortable because of its encompassing pressure on us, and partially blind because it blurs our vision. If we're focused downwards, we see only depths darkening into the unknown. To turn contemplatively into our inner silence is like rising through the surface to encounter the sky. A whole new world opens up as we meet the brilliant sun and fresh air. I think we're often like people who have forgotten that they were made to breathe that air. We're stuck underwater, holding our spiritual breaths or else drowning in a world in which we don't belong. That world isn't, as the Neoplatonists would have us believe, the material or physical world. That world is good and beautiful. Rather, where we don't belong is the busy and chaotic reality of our own making – a place where silence is too often our enemy as we scramble after new distractions.

-o0o-

We live in an increasingly loud world where the din of modernity is almost impossible to elude. This fact has been highlighted by Gordon Hempton, an acoustic ecologist who searched America for one place where he could stand for fifteen minutes without hearing man-made noise. Eventually, he located a spot in Olympia National Forest in Washington State and subsequently fought to have flights diverted to preserve its natural quiet. His account of his search, *One Square Inch of Silence: One Man's Quest to Preserve Quiet*, illustrates how inescapable human noise pollution has become.

> Our cities, our suburbs, our farm communities, even our most expansive and remote national parks are not free from human noise intrusions. Nor is there relief even at the North Pole; continent-hopping jets see to that. Moreover, fighting noise is not the same as preserving silence. Our typical anti-noise strategies – earplugs, noise cancellation headphones, even noise abatement

law – offer no real solution because they do nothing to help us reconnect and listen to the land. And the land is speaking.[8]

The planet pulsates with the hubbub of humanity. The cause of almost all this racket are machines and transportation systems. We've become so adept at tuning out noise pollution that we often recognize it only when we're compelled to confront it like I did when perched atop Craig Lwyd. Often, it's only in places where mechanical clatter is incongruous that we finally notice it. I was struck by this while praying in Brecon Cathedral one afternoon. The doors were shut, and I was alone in that cavernous space, separated from the outside world by thick walls of ancient stone. And yet, as I settled into my contemplation, I gradually realized that the small chapel where I sat wasn't truly quiet – inside, the constant soft hum of the electrical lights and outside, the regular *whoosh* of passing cars accompanied my prayers in a parodic chant. During the early days of the lockdown caused by Covid-19, Brecon once again fell silent and I appreciated just how fortunate were the monks who prayed in our cathedral long before the advent of electricity and engines.

Human clamour has reached such decibels that some birds are now stressed into exhibiting PTSD-like symptoms while others have to shout their mating songs so loudly that they lose the necessary nuances for attracting mates. You try to be a smooth talker when stressed, and forced to yell words of love. We're making the habitat of songbirds like a nightclub for overstressed workers or the performance of *Nessum dorma* in a construction site. Even in the vast ocean silence our machines confuse whale song, causing those mighty beasts to beach themselves or misinterpret mating calls. Other than waste, perhaps nothing characterizes our lives more than noise pollution.

And yet, complain as we do, we embrace sound whenever possible and continually develop new technologies to access it wherever possible. Often when I'm hiking, I pass people listening to music through earbuds that block out the gentle sounds of nature they've presumably gone out of their way to enjoy. I've even been

---

[8]Gordon Hempton and John Grossmann, *One Square Inch of Silence: One Man's Quest for Silence* (New York: Free Press, 2009), 1.

on mountaintops when the blaring booming of a digital music
player has echoed across the rocks and ruined people's peaceful
enjoyment. And I'm no better than anyone else: I usually have
the news pouring into my earholes when walking the dogs in the
morning and music when out running. I'm increasingly of the view
that music has become a debilitating bane of our times – we don't
enjoy it so much as depend on it to rescue us from our greatest fear:
boredom.

We need boredom like we need sleep. Quietness gives our brain
a chance to process experiences and sort out emotions. Periods of
boredom also train us to use our minds in different ways or, at least,
not to be perpetually searching, concentrating, gathering, analysing,
worrying and never resting. Without boredom, our brains become
exhausted, too weary to engage openly and creatively with the
world or process our feelings when they arise. As with God in the
act of creation, our minds need a Sabbath rest. As Norman Wirzba
notes, 'what is at stake in Sabbath observance is not simply that we
manage to pause and refuel enough to continue on in our frantic
and sometimes destructive ways. The real issue is whether we can
learn to see, and then welcome, the divine presence wherever we
are.'[9] These silent Sabbaths are our only opportunities to deal with
ourselves and encounter God, who speaks in a 'still, small voice'.

Through most of his writings, the twentieth-century contemplative
Thomas Merton encouraged people to embrace silence and solitude:
in effect, to delight in monotony. Indeed, he believed that only in
such silent spaces can we find and embrace our true personhood:

> The world of men has forgotten the joys of silence, the peace of
> solitude which is necessary, to some extent, for the fullness of
> human living. Not all men are called to be hermits, but all men
> need enough silence and solitude in their lives to enable the deep
> inner voice of their own true self to be heard at least occasionally.
> When that inner voice is not heard, when man cannot attain to
> the spiritual peace that comes from being perfectly at one with
> his own true self, his life is always miserable and exhausting. For
> he cannot go on happily for long unless he is in contact with the

[9]Norman Wirzba, *Living the Sabbath: Discovering the Rhythms of Rest and Delight*
(Grand Rapids: Brazos Press, 2006), 23–4.

springs of spiritual life which are hidden in the depths of his own soul. If man is constantly exiled from his own home, locked out of his own spiritual solitude, he ceases to be a true person. He no longer lives as a man. He becomes a kind of automaton, living without joy because he has lost his spontaneity. He is no longer moved from within, but only from outside himself.[10]

Far from heeding Merton's advice, we have found new ways to remain in spiritual exile, creating a vast ocean of entertainment and distractions between our fabricated realities and our true homeland. There are far too many cross-currents, whirlpools and eddies of distraction and noise for us to ever cross that ocean. And so, we wither spiritually, falling deaf to the silent world around us and the silent God who loves us – we never pause long enough to discover new depths within ourselves.

Without silence there's also no opportunity to nurture and nourish our social roots, to reflect quietly and even dreamily about our loves and the lives we share with others. We become fixated on the novel and the stimulating – in short, the planned and fabricated world we access in our homes, shops and media. We lose touch with the natural world, fall out of step with its rhythms and harmonies and lose any enduring sense (as we've seen) of belonging to the places where we live. We become like featureless suburbia that can exist anywhere without really belonging to the landscapes on which they're imposed. Perhaps we're doomed to become like the places we inhabit; or perhaps the places we now build manifest our empty selves.

-o0o-

The Christian tradition has long recognized the need for silence. In the Old Testament, we're shown the evocative scene when Elijah is commanded to climb Mt Horeb because the Lord is about to 'pass by'. From the mouth of a cave at the summit, the prophet finds himself amid a series of cataclysms: a wind so ferocious it breaks mountains and cracks rock, then an earthquake and, finally, fire.

---

[10]Thomas Merton, *The Silent Life* (New York: Farrar, Straus & Giroux, 1957), 166–7.

Surely, these are signs of God's presence. This is what readers are disposed to believe, even more so in the original ancient context. But then we're told, 'the Lord was not in the wind', 'the Lord was not in the earthquake', and 'the Lord was not in the fire'. Where is he then? In the Authorized Version, he is heard in a 'still, small voice'. A poetic image to be sure but another one is to be found in a modern translation: 'in the sheer sound of silence'.

Jesus himself regularly withdrew to deserted places to escape from the clamour of human need to be alone with the Father in prayer. The forty days he spent in the wilderness after his baptism were largely days of silence, except for those distracting occasions when Satan appeared to tempt him. Surely, even those diabolical temptations came in the form of an inward dialogue rather than the actual appearance of the devil. If so, then just like us, in the silence of solitude Jesus encountered within himself the inner struggle with vice and virtue that's our common human experience. More often, however, Jesus 'strategically withdraws' into desert places to get away from the crowds and be alone with the Father.[11] At times, these moments of silence echo those of the Old Testament: a re-enactment of Moses, Elijah and even Israel in their solitude. Finally, it was in the silence of his own anguish in a dark and quiet garden that Christ accepted his coming passion and the strength to say, 'Your will not mine be done.'

Likewise, the Desert Fathers escaped into the Egyptian wilderness to wrestle with demons and contemplate God in the vast silence of that desert. Out of that silent land was born Christian monasticism, which welded Christian belief with Platonic mysticism to create a heady brew of asceticism, contemplation and disciplined order. The earliest monks in Egypt were followed by others in the Syrian Desert, and their descendants sought silence in remote monasteries and hermitages, atop high pillars and in the seclusion of their own cells. In the later Middle Ages, Carthusians and Anchorites embraced lives of silence epitomized by the statute for cloistered monks:

> The primary application of our vocation is to give ourselves to the silence and solitude of the cell. It is holy ground, the area

---

[11]Diarmaid MacCulloch, *Silence: A Christian History* (London: Penguin, 2014), 38.

where God and his servant hold frequent conversations, as between friends. There, the soul often unites itself to the Word of God, bride to the groom, the earth to the sky, man to the divine.[12]

Here and elsewhere, the Christian tradition implicitly gives voice to the fact that we're fundamentally creatures of silence. You may find this hard to accept if you're a chatterbox (or are surrounded by them), but even the most garrulous among us are essentially creatures of silence.

I can no more see or hear your thoughts than you can mine. The person who is you – both the one you think you are because of the incessant thoughts that fill your mind and the one who's lurking in the silent depths of your soul – exists in your inner self. That person is unknowable to others unless you communicate. Yet, even were you to spend every minute of your life talking about yourself, you wouldn't be able to express yourself entirely, not least because so much that lurks in our souls remains hidden even from our view. We can't really ever be completely conscious of the deep wells of our 'self', except perhaps in the way that the waters we draw from those wells – our views, habits, decisions, reactions, emotional responses and disposition – seem so hard to change, like trying to freshen water from the tap rather than its source.

The irony about our inner selves is that the more time we spend trying to focus on and express who we think we are, the less we usually remain or become truly ourselves. Since our words can be means of deceit, what we often tell others about us is compromised by what we believe or want to believe about ourselves. Self-interest is a shrewd interpreter. Consequently, words obscure as much as communicate who we are. To an extent, we all join together in a masquerade where we accept each other's masks for real faces. This is why self-absorbed people are generally the most self-deceived, and those most obsessed with their own identities so often end up play-acting.

Moreover, our inner self is as an ocean in comparison to what we want or are able to communicate. How little of ourselves we share even when we're not hampered by our inhibitions. Our

---

[12]'Statutes of Carthusian monks', 4.1. https://www.chartreux.org/en/carthusian-way .php, accessed 27 November 2020.

spoken words consist of only a small part of our whole selves
engaged in our exchanges. This is obvious when we're asked how
we're doing and we reply 'fine', though, truthfully, we could spend
a good hour answering that greeting properly. But it's also true
whenever we speak. That part of us engaging with others is small.
We normally wade only into the shoals of ourselves with hardly a
glance at the depths that lie further in. Indeed, were we unable to
communicate, there would be no evidence of the incredible lives
that exist within us. All the thoughts, feelings, ideas, ponderings,
anxieties, fears, desires and delights that fill our hearts and minds
would remain utterly beyond the knowledge of others. Some might
even be tempted to say that they don't exist. It's striking how similar
our questions about the thoughts of people in a vegetative state
resemble our musings about God.

In fact, this inner silence is one way we bear the image of God.
That unsearchable silence that the faithful recognize as God is the
only thing that we ever encounter that's like the unfathomable
silence we know to be ourselves: a silence that speaks of intellect
and life. Both our inner silence and God's silence call us into their
depths, to discover ourselves in their embrace. In this sense, they
communicate by their very silence. The moment we step away from
the noise of our world, both silences announce themselves loudly
and we find it difficult not to respond. The heart begins its search
with a yearning for something indescribable, even ineffable, that
keeps us from resting in the shallowness of words and noise. We find
that only by responding to that desire can we find peace. And so, we
respond, and in so doing soon glimpse a new reality that can't be
articulated but that we know to be true – truer than anything else
we know. And that knowledge is akin to love.

Silence, though, isn't the end. Neither we nor God is silence
itself. Rather, we must enter into the 'silent land' to discover the
personalities – ours and God's – that no words can communicate.
The anonymous fourteenth-century author of the *Cloud of
Unknowing* writes:

> For silence is not God, nor is speaking God; fasting is not God,
> nor is eating God; being alone is not God, nor is company
> God; nor yet any one of every such pair of contraries. He is hid
> between them; and he cannot be found by any work of your
> soul, but only by the love of your heart. He cannot be thought,

grasped, or searched out by the understanding. But he can be loved and chosen by the true and loving desire of your heart.[13]

Notice that all that is said here of God is true of people, too. We are more than the sum total of our interactions with others, even our most intimate acquaintances. We are hidden between them like the silence between notes.

Without some notion of the divine, existence can become intolerably solitary. Scholars have often noted the sour note of distance, isolation and alienation in modern literature and art. Edvard Munch's *The Scream*, which expresses the anxiety of modern solitude, has become an icon of our age. We're disposed in our individualistic society to accentuate the distances that lie between us. Here, I think, we see that the true fruit of individualism isn't personal freedom and happiness but dreary estrangement. Standing apart from others and even from our shared natural world, we end up standing apart from ourselves and living what amounts to a fretful and distracted existence.

But when our silent selves stretch out towards the silent God, we find life and purpose in the commingling of silences. God's silence can and does speak into our own silence, filling that inward loneliness with his own presence. The Welsh poet-priest R. S. Thomas tries to capture this in one of his poems:

But the silence in the mind
is when we live best, within
listening distance of the silence
we call God. This is the deep
calling to deep of the psalm-
writer, the bottomless ocean . . .
It is a presence, then,
whose margins are our margins;
that calls us out over our
own fathoms . . .[14]

[13]*The Assessment of Inner Stirrings* in *The Pursuit of Wisdom and Other Words, by the Author of The Cloud of Unknowing*, ed. S. J. James Walsh (New York: Paulist Press, 1988), 140.
[14]R. S. Thomas, 'AD', *Counterpoint* (Hexham: Bloodaxe Books Ltd, 1990).

This is what contemplation within the Christian tradition really is: the deliberate act of withdrawing into our own quiet souls so that we can reach out in love to encounter the eternal silence of God. That ascent, I would add, requires us also to put ourselves in the presence of the world's own stillness – apart from distracting sounds and captivating sights – so that we can dwell in a trinity of silence: that of God, self and creation. Within the silence of creation, our silent selves enter into the 'silent land' where we discover our silent God.

The human world doesn't know the mystery of that silence, though people yearn for it. It's a deep silence that we recognize not only as the ground of our own being but also as the goal of all our strivings – it's a silence that the great mystics have also recognized as love. In the words of the twelfth-century monk William of St-Thierry: 'O you who are true Love, the love-worthy Lord, this . . . is the will of your Son in us, this is his prayer for us to you the Father: "I will that, as you and I are one, so may they themselves be one in us." This is the goal, this is the consummation, this is perfection, this is peace, this is the "joy of the Lord", this is joy in the Holy Spirit, this is the "silence of heaven".'[15] In other words, when we withdraw into the silence of the world and into the deep silence of our own souls, we encounter the silence that communicates God and discover that all those silences are one and the same – the presence of Love, that divine love that underpins all things and draws them all to their Creator. Such deep silence is therefore like the silence shared between two lovers or a mother and her newborn, that speaks more loudly than any words of endearment.

---

[15]William of St-Thierry, *On Contemplating God*, VIII, in *On Contemplating God, Prayer, Meditations*, trans. C. S. M. V. Penelope Lawson (Kalamazoo: Cistercian Press, 1970), 48.

6

Gwyn ap Nudd

Words

I'm a bit of a connoisseur of old stories. When I was young, I delighted in Celtic and Norse myths and, later, in those odd, charming folktales that offer no moral beyond the pleasure of a good yarn. The more whimsical the tale, the better, especially in the case of those that purport to be true. I don't even mind if these supposedly true accounts are completely fanciful – like the one about twentieth-century planners who diverted a new road around a fungal fairy ring because the locals feared invoking a curse. I suspect it never happened, and yet I've now heard it retold at least three times in entirely different contexts.

When I was in second grade, this love for a good yarn would get me into trouble at school. Even though I was a painfully shy boy, I couldn't abide not being called up by the teacher to speak during 'Show n' tell'. For some reason, this didn't encourage me to actually take something into school to show the class. Instead, I fabricated stories and claimed they were true. But I couldn't calibrate my wild imagination – I have a vague recollection of once spinning a yarn about hunting sharks underwater and becoming quite indignant with my sceptical classmates. I don't think these awkward flights of fancy were some incredibly inept attempt to get people to like me more. I just wanted to tell a good story, often to the despair of my long-suffering teacher.

Standing in the landscapes where legends and folktales were set is an unforgettable experience. Walking where their characters walked and breathing the same air that they breathed are the closest we can come to entering Narnia or Middle Earth. Such an encounter between the imagination and landscape struck me very powerfully a few years ago when I backpacked on the Laugavegur Trail in central Iceland. The walk during the first few days was spectacular, immersed as we were in the technicolour of grey rock, sandstone, bright red and orange soils, and grass in shades of green I thought impossible in nature. On my final morning, I climbed to the top of a height in Thórsmörk across a broad, grey river valley from the infamous Eyjafjallajökull volcano that wreaked havoc on air traffic in 2009. From there, I looked across another broad river basin at the little homesteads dotting the opposing, desolate slopes. I held in one hand my map and in the other my battered copy of *Njal's Saga*, which had been given to me by my Latin teacher in high school. *Njal's Saga* is an enthralling tale of love, violence, loyalty and generational feuds set in Viking Iceland over a thousand years ago. From my vantage, I could look at the rudimentary map at the beginning of the book, find the same names on my twenty-first-century map and pick out in the landscape in front of me a few of the isolated homesteads they denoted. I was standing on the periphery of a saga's world, seeing with my own eyes the setting of those ancient legends. It gave me goosebumps.

Of course, I don't have to go to Iceland for that kind of experience. I often walk with my wife and dogs to nearby Llyn y Fan Fach, a dark lake set beneath the soaring green slopes of the Carmarthen Fans on the western edges of the Brecon Beacons. It's a popular spot that can now be reached by a gravel road that meanders between craggy hills along a dark stream notched by the white water of low falls. If you go there on a warm, sunny day, you'll encounter a small army of walkers and picnickers at the shore of the lake, often with children skipping stones along the otherwise still waters. How many know, I often wonder, that this isn't any old lake – it's the home of the Lady in the Lake.

No, not *that* Lady – not the one who lobs swords as the basis for a form of government. She's another Lady, who lived in the murky waters of Llyn y Fan Fach and became the object of a boy's abiding love. In this tale, she offers herself in marriage to him when he becomes a man, but with a promise and a warning: love her and he will gain a great fortune but strike her three times and she will return to the lake forever. These tales always work out the same way: as soon as the young man is warned, we know it'll happen. And so back she goes into the cold lake, leaving her dejected husband so broken and remorseful that he soon dies. A sad story but with a happier variation in which they have a child who later visits the lake in search of his mother. According to local tradition, he finds her there and, during his regular visits, is taught by her the art of healing, which he then teaches others – a group of actual doctors called the Physicians of Myddfai who lived during the Middle Ages. Fairy tale elides into history in Wales within a landscape one can explore in a morning or afternoon.

-o0o-

As with paper or parchment, words must be inscribed into such landscapes in order for them to tell tales. A sheet or paper lying on a table is obviously a silent object. Unless you rattle it in the air or rub it against the table's surface, it makes no sound. But just add ink in the shape of letters and the page erupts into spoken life. It can tell stories, recite poetry, sing songs, inform, berate, flatter and break or melt hearts. And once inscribed onto these silent pages, the words take on a degree of permanence. They've been captured, grasped from the air before they can fade away and pinned down so they can't escape. Writing is not unlike bottling the sound of the wind: just as magical, too, if we're whimsical enough to recognize it.

Landscapes are the same. We've already seen this in the first part of this book. What is thick-history but words and stories inscribed into a landscape? Our words breathe such spaces into storied life, imbuing them with history and slowly laying down new layers of affection and meaning. We humans have probably always treated the landscapes in which we find ourselves as blank pages on which to write our stories. We've been writing our shared stories onto them far longer than we have on paper, populating them with tales of ancestors, gods, heroes and monsters. We glimpse such stories not only in the Old Testament but also in works like Virgil's *Aeneid* and Livy's *Founding of Rome*, the *Mabinogion* in Wales and the *Kalevala* of Finland. The world abounds with early examples of stories born of earth, tree and rock.

Cadair Idris is no different: its monumental silence has produced a wealth of words.

First, there are the myths and legends associated with the mountain. The mighty giant Idris Gawr is said to have enjoyed reclining on Cwm Cau to admire the stars. According to one legend, he was actually Idris the Coarse, who spent his time picking irritating boulders from between his massive toes and flinging them down the mountain where they remain to this day. But the story that has stuck is that he visits those who spend the night on Cadair Idris either to strike them mad or make them poets, which admittedly can often be the same thing. When I tell people about my spending the night on Cadair Idris, if they ask me about my poetry or sanity, then I know they're probably from Wales.[1]

According to another old myth, Cadair Idris is the hunting ground of Gwyn ap Nudd, the old Fairy King and ruler of Annwn, the otherworld of Welsh mythology. Like those of many figures in Welsh mythology and legend, the stories about Gwyn aren't systematic – in some he's one of King Arthur's knights, in others a fairy and in still others more like a pagan god. In some, he's a force for good who gathers the souls of the valiant Welsh dead, while elsewhere he's a more sinister character. His association with Cadair Idris is generally of the latter sort. It is said that the mountain is the territory for the wild hunt of his fearsome hounds who roam its slopes in search of souls to drag back to Annwn. Their howl portends death should you have the misfortune to hear it. So, if Idris doesn't get you, Gwyn's hounds very well might.

A more light-hearted old story about Cadair Idris concerns Morgan ap Rhys, who one evening is enjoying his 'pipe and his pot and had become, through his frequent libations to the jolly god, rather extra good humoured and merry'. Suddenly, there's a knock on his door and in walk three fairies disguised as travellers. Like any good Welshmen, Morgan offers them a meal and a drink and is rewarded by the grateful fairies with a magical 'harp to play a merry tune'. So thrilled is Morgan by his gift that he runs to the village pub to play for his friends. As soon as he begins to strum the strings, everyone springs up and starts dancing frantically 'as if they had lost their intellects, some so high, that had there been no roof to the house, God knows where they would have gone; at least one would suppose they wanted to visit the man in the moon'. Thereafter, whenever Morgan is in his cups, he begins to

---

[1]For those wondering, I've camped overnight on Cadair Idris twice without any improvement to my poetry.

play and the people to dance, 'which did considerable damage to the good folk of the neighbourhood, many of whom had their limbs dislocated'. Eventually, the harp mysteriously disappears, the fairies having retrieved it from Morgan out of compassion for the villagers. For me, this story epitomizes the genius of fairy tales: whimsical without a drop of moralism.[2]

There are other legends, too, as stories cling to Cadair Idris like the flocks that graze upon it. People today retell one about the stone in the Dysynni Valley mentioned earlier on, which are etched generations of shepherds' names. The stone also contains an imprint shaped like a hoof long deemed to be that of the devil who chased away young ne'er-do-wells who gathered there to dance instead of going to chapel. Awfully considerate and pious of Old Scratch, I would say.

Cadair Idris also includes Christian stories: like that of the Breton St Cadfan who founded an early monastery by the sea at the bottom of the Dysynni Valley. Cadfan is one of the great saints of early Wales and is said to have founded the monastery on the Isle of Bardsey that lies off the Llyn Peninsula and later became the burial place of Welsh royalty and (it is said) 20,000 saints. A pre-Viking stone monument still stands in a local parish church; on it are inscribed the earliest written words of Welsh in dedication to deceased loved ones. But, of course, the enduring stories are those that came *from* Cadfan's little monastery: the Gospel preached to the people living nearby that would produce over time other churches like the one I had found in Llanfihangel-y Pennant. Funny to think that Idris flinging boulders, Gwyn hunting souls, the devil chasing off misbehaving youth and Christ redeeming souls bump shoulders in the landscape of Cadair Idris. All are perhaps in danger of being forgotten, too.

Other stories are more recent but equally evocative such as that of Mary Jones trekking to Bala to get her Welsh Bible. That story still inspires people living not only in the vicinity of her home but also throughout the world to go to re-enact her mountainous trek to Bala. Such is the power of the stories of Cadair Idris that even Nonconformists, not generally known for their veneration of

[2]W. Howells, *Cambrian Superstitions, Comprising Ghosts, Omens, Witchcraft, Traditions, &c* (London: Longman & Co., 1831), 150–2.

holy shrines, are for a time transformed into pious pilgrims. Like charcoal and sulphur added to saltpetre, words and stories are explosive when inscribed onto spectacular landscapes.

Just as the Hebrew Bible contains myths, folk stories, histories, poems, prophecies and proverbs from many different times, so too has Cadair Idris accumulated its own parade of prose and poetry. These stories sit alongside each other in the landscape, each providing a new layer of narrative that enchants the hills and valleys with human life. One of the things I like about such stories is that they depend on their landscapes – they can't pretend to stand outside them like our stories often do. They're too earthed for that, as though their rich soil runs through the veins of their characters.

What do I mean by this? What are our shared stories these days? I can think of specific ones like Star Wars and Harry Potter that derive from film, television and mass-produced books. Increasingly, gaming worlds are generating new stories that people share around the globe. These are particularly evocative because of the agency that's given to the audience. You don't just have to listen to a set story, you can now explore it with a flick of the wand we call a gaming console. As I have noted elsewhere, almost all the stories today that spark children's imaginations are of this kind.[3] Flickering screens have replaced fireside stories and even books; our storytellers are no longer primarily the people we know and love, and who, in the retelling, imbue and embellish their stories with their own personality. Now, they're distant faceless people subject more to the whims of a wide market than to people sharing a common land and heritage.

One of the key features of our stories these days is transportability. They must be crafted, or recrafted, in a way that can appeal and be sold to anyone in the world. Disney mastered this process long ago, reworking old folktales like Cinderella, Sleeping Beauty and Aladdin into global vehicles for affluent western moralities and commodities. The landscape and folk traditions that originally inspired them are preserved only as exotic backdrops for characters otherwise more comfortable in California than in their original setting. We don't retell old stories so much as strip mine them to produce profitable goods for the consumption of global imaginations. Tellingly, these

---

[3] See my *Rescuing the Church from Consumerism* (London: S.P.C.K., 2013), 24–5.

stories even produce their own waste: the cheap, plastic toys that are destined for our landfills or to be washed up on our beaches. Moreover, we're now too mobile for local stories to endure. We need those told on television and in mass-produced books because we no longer have stories organically produced in the places where we live. If we're lucky enough to grow up in one place, we may hear tales about the recently deceased or the history of local houses and shops:

> I remember when the laundromat was old Mr Brown's General Store. It had the best selection of sweets . . .
> That's where Mrs. Vitriol used to live. You didn't want to get on the wrong side of her . . .

These kinds of stories are often embellished in the retelling and not infrequently nostalgic. They're our last vestige of the kind of oral tradition that stretched back generations out of mind. But it's hard to hear such stories among the clamour of mass entertainment and it's impossible for them to sink their hooks into us when we refuse to stand still long enough to listen to them. No, the stories we enjoy today are like our cars and computers – portable and easily reproduced in a million different forms.

In contrast, old, local stories reflect their landscapes by sharing in their strange juxtaposition of timelessness and thick time. They're rooted in particular places and historical contexts and yet they enjoy universal appeal because they deal with human beings. A shared humanity allows me to identify with Penelope longing for Odysseus's return, or Hrothgar despairing over his inability to protect his people from Grendal's cruel menace or Elizabeth Bennet working through her feelings about Mr Darcy. None of these were written with me in mind. Their authors could know nothing about the tastes and opinions of a twenty-first-century middle-aged American. And yet I can identify with their characters. Seeing myself in strange characters in foreign, even mythical, settings reminds me that there is a deep, underlying human condition that no culture or span of time can obscure or change. Old stories introduce us to people of old in whom we don't find strangers but ourselves. Shakespeare's plays are timeless even if their setting and words aren't.

Yet these stories are also rooted in the thick-history from which they arose. Penelope is every inch an ancient Greek, Hrothgar an early medieval Dane and Elizabeth a gentrified young lady of Regency England. Their settings aren't just convenient backdrops for characters and plots but the essence of the stories themselves. By entering into those characters through my imagination and seeing their world through their eyes, I step out of my own time and glimpse what it was like to live in theirs. Without these stories we wouldn't even have a notion of past ages. We really know about Greek culture, morality, prejudices, virtues and sensibilities only because we can enter into their stories and wade in the shoals of their now vanished thick-history.

Notice what happens when landscapes, timelessness and thick-history meld together in stories. I can encounter unlikely people in distant ages and within specific landscapes – say Morgan ap Rhys greeting his fairy wayfarers on his doorstep near Cadair Idris – and, yet, still identify with them deeply and often movingly. On the face of it, this shouldn't be possible so foreign are such people to us. Morgan's early modern world (or, really, that of the tale's author) and my late modern one couldn't be more different. We congratulate ourselves on how advanced we've become and celebrate the cultural and moral chasm that lies between us and the benighted people of bygone eras. And yet when I read the stories from the far side of that chasm, it's not only possible for me to identify with their characters, but it's also almost impossible for me *not to do so*. No matter how foreign, strange and even repugnant their setting and views may be, they are my imaginative neighbours rather than incomprehensible strangers. In a culture that often encourages us to identify ourselves *against* others, stories continue to invite us to identify ourselves *with* them. Thus, stories teach us to be humane by training us to recognize the familiar in everyone, no matter how odd or off-putting their beliefs and opinions may be.

-o0o-

The old myths, legends and stories that find their home on and around Cadair Idris form the storied backdrop to all the private and local stories that chart the lives of people and villages there. Idris, Gwyn ap Nudd, St Cadfan, Morgan ap Rhys, Mary Jones and countless others remain like familiar neighbours to at least some of the people who for generations have called that place home. They may not be as well remembered or as often conjured back into life by storytellers as in the past, but they still lurk near enough for even a visiting American to meet them during his brief visits.

Those myths, legends, poems and stories imbue the mountain with personality. Cadair Idris isn't just a massive hunk of rock rising above the sea and forming the southern rim of the Harlech Dome; it's a particular mountain storied into a particular place within Welsh folklore and history. It is the giant Idris's Chair, King's Arthur's Seat, the hunting ground of Gwyn ap Nudd, the backdrop to St Cadfan's monastery and the mountain that young Mary Jones crossed to buy her Bible – it's also the stage for countless stories (probably no less exaggerated) told by climbers to impress friends and strangers alike.

I've been struck by this last point whenever I've led retreats or given talks about my mountaintop reflections. Invariably here in the UK, there are one or two people who have climbed to Cadair's summit, or even spent the night by Llyn Cau or in the bothy at the top. They can't help but approach me after my talk to share their experiences – usually involving rain, fog and mud – and by doing so add their modest story to all the others I've heard or read. The summit of many mountains here in Britain are marked by cairns, piles of stones gradually erected by people to mark the end of their climb. Each climber adds a new stone until a mound of rock – some quite ancient – stands like a sentinel in the mountain landscape. The tales I'm told about Cadair Idris are like this: each person adding his/her own personal account to those of others, gradually building (as it were) a cairn of stories in my mental landscape. How many such stories are retold every year by people who visit and are enraptured by what they see, hear and feel? Our compulsion to describe beautiful places to others transforms visual wonders into audible ones.

Places like Cadair Idris also remind us that words and landscapes once intersected. Wales is filled with examples of this: the many *llans* that memorialize venerated saints or holy sites of the distant past – Llanfair, Llandaff, Llanbedr, and (under the care of Brecon Cathedral), Llanddew, where Gerald of Wales once lived and the ruins of his palace still remain. If they're not named after holy sites or saints, Welsh place names refer to topographical features, which can be quite precise like the top of a mountain (*pen*), a slope (*rhiw*) or the mouth of a river (*avon*). One of the most evocative I've come across is Rhiwsaeson, now just a hamlet slowly being absorbed into the greater conurbation of Cardiff. In English, it means something like

'Slope of the Saxons' and obviously refers to a nearby hill crowned by an ancient hill fort where I used to walk my dog regularly. I don't believe anyone is certain about the origin of its name. Why is it named after the hated *Saes*, the invading Saxons of old who drove the Welsh out of much of Britain? One theory is that it's the site of an old battle between the Welsh and the English, but we don't really know because the words surrounding that name have vanished into the past like the hill fort into the pasture where sheep now graze.

Landscapes underpin the words we use. That's why mythological lore is deliberately placed within familiar landscapes – the *Odyssey* and the *Aeneid* are good examples – imbuing those locations with significance. Stonehenge and Avebury sit within a ritual landscape, the Parthenon perches high on a promontory overlooking Athens, the Greek gods dwell atop Mt Olympus and many ancient British churches stand near holy wells or other sacred sites. In Britain, archaeological finds and ancient legends suggest a now-lost world where myth and environment were almost indistinguishable; groves, high hills, pools, marshland, springs, islands and the sea populated the mythic imaginary of the people of that world. Not far from my house, in a small village called Defynnog stands a medieval church that contains an inscribed stone from post-Roman Britain. A remarkably old place – but young compared to the yew tree in its churchyard, which may be over 5,000 years old and may have been considered sacred before Rome was even a dream.

Similarly, our own landscapes carry and sustain our words: shopping malls, cinemas, the open road, sports stadiums, beach resorts and sprawling housing estates underpin much of our contemporary language, enabling us to understand what people mean when they speak of values, fame, freedom, excitement, leisure and relaxation, and even home. Our commercial landscapes foster our hopes and dreams as well as our fears and taboos. In all cases, the environment in which people live shapes the stories and practices that form the background to their lives and help to conjure an imaginary that informs how they perceive the world to which they belong. This process is organic, as well, connecting people to their landscapes as handed-down words are gathered like crops into stories, rituals and practices.

In that sense, words allow our landscapes to speak us into existence. From words, we build the communities and civilizations to which we belong. The exchange of words is the vehicle for expressing our loves and hopes and for weaving together that sense of identity that has become the peculiar obsession of our times. But these words are not grabbed from the ether; they arise from our encounter with our home landscapes, which provide the soil in which our more abstract ideas can take root and blossom. If you really want to get people to think and speak differently, then you have to begin by uprooting them from their landscapes. With the notable exception of Jewish and Armenian narratives, our cultural stories are like plants that quickly wither when yanked from their native soil. The Romans who destroyed Druidic groves, Christians who tore down pagan temples, Protestants who pulled down monasteries and ISIS fighters who demolished non-Sunni Muslim sites understood this well. Consumer culture is even now transforming our own landscapes, thus reshaping our language, and so, too, us.

-oOo-

Words and landscapes breathe life into the Christian faith. Most obviously, we have the sacred words contained in Scripture: the words that provide the substance of our faith, which teach us about the God we worship, the people to whom we belong and the hope that sustains us. In the phrase of the theologian Stanley Hauerwas, Christians are members of a 'story-formed' community: the words of Scripture demarcate us from the rest of the world and enable us to understand what it means to be and to believe.

No words have had greater impact than those found in the Bible. Almost all the most deeply cherished beliefs of even our secular society find their origin there. The words of Scripture gave us our ideas about personal agency, equality, the rule of law, care for the poor, justice and mercy, the exercise of authority and the limits of warfare (among other things). They comforted enslaved Africans and gave words of fire to abolitionists and civil rights activists. They stirred the colonies to throw off monarchical power and envision a Republic in which everyone (or eventually everyone) had the right to 'life, liberty, and the pursuit of happiness'. Undoubtedly, the Bible has also been used to oppress, do violence and close minds, but that again just shows its power. We are who we are because of the roughly 750,000 words found between the *In the beginning* of Genesis and the *Amen* of Revelation.

Many churches also have the words of the liturgy that enable
congregations to worship as one, often using prayers crafted in long-
vanished and forgotten places. Those words, phrases and prayers
express the diverse experiences of the church, in effect allowing the
voices of our dead ancestors to pray through our living throats.
For example, within the Church of England on the Fourth Sunday
before Lent, congregations join in a prayer of protection that reads:

> O God, you know us to be set in the midst of so many and great
> dangers, that by reason of the frailty of nature we cannot always
> stand upright: grant to us such strength and protection as may
> support us in all dangers and carry us through all temptations;
> through Jesus Christ your Son our Lord, who is alive and reigns
> with you, in the unity of the Holy Spirit, one God, now and for
> ever.[4]

Many who pray this today probably think it's invoking divine
assistance amid our fears and anxieties. The words address the
troubles that may press upon us, which is why they're still prayed.
But they were probably composed in the ruin of Roman civilization
for Christians threatened by barbarian invasions – their 'many and
great dangers' were all too real and present. Those words, composed
amid the perilous despair of social collapse, trip lightly off the lips
of comfortable western Christians today. And yet they still speak.

Words also form the basis of Christian preaching; Christianity
is a religion of proclamation, preaching and teaching people about
the life, death and rising of Christ. Such proclamation is inherently a
story, a retelling of the Gospel, the 'Good News' of Christ's ministry.
Indeed, almost all the sermons in the Acts of the Apostles take
the form of stories: the narrative we know as the Old Testament
culminating in the life of Christ. Their words, rooted in the story
of Israel and Jesus, announce God's Kingdom, and expose the dark
recesses of the human heart. 'The word of God is living and active,
sharper than any two-edged sword, piercing to the division of soul
and of spirit, of joints and of marrow, and discerning the thoughts
and intentions of the heart' (Heb. 4.12). The Christian story of
redemption provides the rich soil from which almost all our ideas,

---

[4]Church of England, *Common Worship*, 461.

beliefs and institutions have sprung. Whether we recognize it or not, the ideas of sacrifice and redemption are thus woven inextricably into the fabric of our collective life and reality.

But just as other stories and legends don't spring out of nothing, so too are the words we encounter in the Bible and in our liturgies rooted in landscapes. The language of the Bible constantly invites our imaginations to travel to distant lands: Eden, Egypt, Israel, Judea, a manger in Bethlehem, a cross on a lonely hill, the Roman East and even the heavenly Jerusalem. They draw us into identifying ourselves most fully not with dry concepts or mythological beings, but with fallible people situated for the most part in actual landscapes. Those places lay hold powerfully to how Christians understand where they live. Longings to find or fashion new Edens have occasioned everything from the New England colonies to the Eden Project in Cornwall. Visions about building new Jerusalems inspired reform movements and fired the imagination of poets like William Blake. And the landscapes of Exodus – Egypt, the wilderness, the Promised Land – provided the metaphorical landscape for the costly movement of African Americans from slavery to freedom.

More mundane examples of how biblical landscapes have influenced us are to be found in place names that dot the globe: infamous Salem of Puritanical witch-hunts, Shiloh where Yankees and Confederates once slaughtered each other with hot lead or the mountainous Pisgah Forest near Asheville, North Carolina. Just down the road from my home in Wales is Libanus (the old name for Lebanon), a tiny village in the rain-soaked foothills of the Brecon Beacons which, frankly, looks nothing like its more arid namesake. My father-in-law lives near two villages in north Wales with biblical names: Babell (Welsh for Babel) and Sodom, which have to be among the strangest choices found anywhere.

The Christian liturgy similarly uses words to transport people into new landscapes. Most obviously, the seasons of the church year place worshippers in first-century Palestine among desperate Jews, notorious sinners, conniving clergy, colonizing Romans and a wandering Rabbi making outrageous claims and performing miracles. It's hard to exaggerate the power of this annual time-travel Christians around the globe make to walk alongside Jesus from his birth in a manger to his resurrection from a tomb and ascension to heaven. Liturgical Christians thus spend a great deal of their collective life in an imagined landscape far removed from their own – one they share in a wonderful way with Christians who have gone before them. In fact, that landscape unites Christians – Protestant and Catholic, liberal and conservative, past and present, and of every race and ethnicity – in ways that we probably don't appreciate and celebrate enough.

The liturgy is also conducted in a particular location: a church building. It is, if you will, the language of that place, drawing people through performed words into an enduring metaphorical landscape. Within the space of our church buildings, the liturgy invites movement: not only sitting, kneeling and standing but also approaching the altar. The liturgy divides churches into two metaphorical spaces: the *nave*, which represents the world, and the *sanctuary*, which represents heaven. Thus, when Christians go up to the altar to receive communion, they symbolically ascend to heaven. Likewise, when the Gospel is processed down the aisle amid the congregation, it symbolically descends from heaven into the world. In these ways, words transform church buildings into a microcosm of our world – heaven and earth are metaphorically recreated within their walls so that worshipping congregations become humanity in microcosm gathered, like the four beasts and kings in Revelation, around the heavenly throne in worship to the Lamb of God.

The Bible and our liturgies, therefore, lay the foundation for our life together as a Christian community; communication is, in fact, the basis for all communities. *Communicate, community* and *communion* derive from the same Latin word for 'sharing in common'.[5] If this is true, then Christian landscapes and words engender Christian identities. They breathe us into existence in the same way that other myths breathe life into the civilizations that depend on them. In many ways, our shared stories and landscapes are more enduring than even Christian beliefs. Non-Christians tell their children stories about Noah's Ark or attend church at Christmas to hear again the story of Christ's birth. Similarly, earlier attempts to rationalize Christianity into moral and doctrinal principles have all proved short-lived. In both cases, we're reminded that stories and

---

[5]Oliver O'Donovan, *Common Objects of Love, Moral Reflection and the Shaping of Community: The 2001 Stob Lectures* (Grand Rapids: William B Eerdmans Pub., 2002), 26–7.

their landscapes are what grab our hearts – the imaginary soil they lay down doesn't always produce faith, but without it, Christian beliefs soon wither and decay.

Yet, the Christian message also contains the astonishing claim that words go even deeper into our existence. Central to that claim is the belief that our words, insofar as they contain meaning and can communicate, arise from the eternal Word. Indeed, that Word is the source of existence for everything: 'In the beginning was the Word, and the Word was with God, and the Word was God. . . . All things came into being through him, and without him not one thing came into being' (John 1.1, 2). Our own words are, therefore, only tokens of the eternal Word, through whom all things were made and by whom we have been saved.

Recall Genesis: God didn't just create the world with some silent power or with the flick of a divine wrist. Rather, he said, 'Let there be' and there was: heaven and earth, sun and moon, land and water, and all living things. We are the living syllables of God's speech. Augustine likened creation to a cosmic poem or song, given shape and form by the eternal Word who utters every syllable of creation into being. In short, we're surrounded by words. Out of silence, the Word speaks everything into existence. In that divinely uttered world, we speak ourselves into social existence through the words and stories we share with each other. Only then do we discover ourselves, form our beliefs and formulate our common objects of love. It's as if a singer kept every note of his/her most exquisite aria from echoing away into silence, weaving them together to fashion a world that resounds with his/her beautiful voice.

When you think of it that way, how much more magical are we than a harp conjured by fairies for a lonely farmer on Cadair Idris. Our imagination just requires ears sharp enough to hear it.

7

Baptism

Another paradox: the silence of my evening by the shore of Llyn Cau belied the stories inspired by Cadair Idris's mountainous landscape. Sitting in the darkening bowl of Cwm Cau, I was surrounded by silence: an immense quiet that might feel ominous to many who might sit there alone on a dark night. But generations upon generations of people encountering the massive wildness of that silent mountain have been inspired to weave striking stories from it. Out of that ageless silence have come imaginative and remarkable tales: indeed, the story of Cadair Idris.

Despite those stories, the silence remains. Except where the sounds of human activity can be heard (like those cars on the A-road that had ruined my earlier reverie), that silence is practically ageless. It's the same silence encountered by those who invented the legends and folktales set on or around Cadair Idris – or at least since sheep with their constant bleating were introduced. There's a sound to the world's silence that's hidden behind the hubbub of human life. But there's another silence, too, where the natural world has no stories, where human beings haven't narrated nature with personality, clothing it with its own set of colourful stories and memories. If I hadn't bothered to do some reading first, I would never have known the stories associated with Cadair Idris and consequently would have remained ignorant of its storied personality. The deep drone of the wind just before the next morning's sunrise would not have conjured Gwyn ap Nudd's hounds in my imagination. I wouldn't have known the poetry of the place.

Perhaps this is another way that landscapes are like people. I'm by nature an introvert. Except when I'm wearing my clericals (funny how a uniform can shape behaviour), I'm, in fact, surprisingly bashful when I find myself amid strangers. I was once an incredibly shy, little boy who often hid beneath his mother's skirts. Because I was so shy, I learned to observe people, to use my fleeting glances to study those around me. I would take the measure of their silent selves, watching their movements, expressions, the mindless things they were doing, how they, too, were quietly assessing others. From these I formed an impression, an image of who they were. I now know how misleading those images can be. Even the briefest conversation suddenly adds a new dimension: personality. Out of the silent bodies of others is spoken a person that no amount of observation could have uncovered.

Big cities teach this lesson in abundance: there, we're constantly surrounded by people who are to us like automatons – creatures who move around and even gaze back at us but otherwise exist to us only as animated objects. On those occasions when I take public transport – especially the London Underground – I wonder what personalities lurk within the people avoiding any eye contact as they wend their way from point A to B. In their silence, many of them seem to be a certain kind of person – often their clothes or facial expressions suggest personalities – but as individuals they remain obscure. Hidden in the minds of each person is a rich tapestry of life and personality; sitting somewhere near me on the Underground train is someone who, if only we conversed, might reveal new worlds and ideas, or even change my life. To be relentlessly surrounded by strangers isn't how we're meant to live; it's unhealthy. We need neighbours, people whose stories we know and who know ours. Existential loneliness is the condition of someone unmoored from others – someone who has never really belonged.

We find strangers harder to love. We shouldn't. Jesus' Parable of the Good Samaritan tells us that loving our neighbours as ourselves includes strangers. But he had to tell his parable only because it runs so much against our grain to care for strangers. No, we love our own; however, we define them. Knowing others as persons – allowing them to become our neighbours – disposes us towards being, well, neighbourly. It's the human equivalent of farmers supposedly telling their children not to name the animals they're planning to eat. Personality breathes life and evokes love.

Personality is why conversation is so different from observation. If I take the time to get to know the people I've observed, then their stories and their lives change how I see them. I quickly learn how wrong my first impressions were, that what their silent selves communicated to me had as much to do with me as with what I was seeing. And knowledge of their voiced selves is so powerful that I soon can't recall those first impressions – I can no longer even pretend to see them as strangers because their personalities have transformed them from human objects into human subjects. That transformation wrests control from me: I lose the freedom to see them only as I wish and must submit to what I discover through our new relationship. That new knowledge may not reveal their true selves – all relationships are shaped by degrees of self-deception – but I must now respond as much to their interaction with me as to my observation of them.

Similarly, I now know Cadair Idris in ways I don't know most other mountains because I've encountered its storied personality. I'm very fond of the mountains I once climbed regularly in Pisgah National Forest, but most of them lack this kind of personality. Their character is now almost entirely natural – *of nature* – since any stories that once breathed them into imaginary life are largely forgotten or were erased by the forced removal of the Cherokees who once composed and shared their own stories about them. Many, of course, have taken on new personalities as settlers, farmers, miners, and impoverished Appalachian communities incorporated them into their social imagination. But many more stand silent now, shorn of all stories except those told now by holiday-makers and outdoor enthusiasts.

We have similar places in Wales that were long ago silenced. I have already mentioned Pen-y-crug, a high hill on the northwest border of Brecon atop which are perched the still visible ramparts of an ancient hill fort. What stories must those ancient inhabitants have told one another that were set in the landscapes I now call home? Since people lived there far longer than the United States has existed, I can only assume that the hills, rivers, valleys and mountains that form this part of the Brecon Beacons National Park must have been fertilized with stories numbered beyond reckoning. And not just any stories, but ones that let them know who they and their now utterly forgotten ancestors were. All of them have long since fallen into irrecoverable silence. The landscape has been rewritten with new stories like a computer's operating system installed over an old one. No amount of romanticizing about ancient paganism – never mind attempts to recreate it – can retrieve them. When words fall silent and memory fades, stories vanish forever.

History contains a melancholic irony: the very scarcity of its sources underscores the vast oceans of human experiences now beyond the reach of historians. What we no longer remember about our past far exceeds what we do. Historians of the ancient world are constantly confronted by this fact. Their studies draw our attention to all the memories and experiences that have been forever lost: entire civilizations reduced to a few clay tablets and a few scraps of literature. I don't see how archaeologists resist falling into a deep melancholy, knowing that beneath the dust they scrape away lie the stories of people whom the finality of death and forgetting have silenced.

The remarkable and unique stories of the dead are gone. We remember only the highlights of the high and mighty – and only some of them – and can never know what inspirations, fears, prejudices, longings, insights, motives and personalities were once carried in the thoughts and words of the vast number of people who draw breath no longer. 'Remember that you are dust and to dust you will return.' That could just as easily have been written, 'Remember that you were silence and to silence you will return.'

I'm often reminded of this mournful fact when I walk around Brecon Cathedral or through the churchyard. The floor of the cathedral was paved in the nineteenth century by the famous architect George Gilbert Scott using the old memorial stones that marked our dead with strikingly etched fonts. I frequently stop to read one or two of them when I'm in the cathedral and reflect on the lives of those they name. Likewise, each morning when I walk the dogs, I cross through a forest of graves, weathering away in the moist Welsh air, that mark the burial places of the forgotten dead. The memorials and graves are inscribed with the barest details of those for whom they were made; in fact, many of those outside have been weather-worn into illegibility. Those lives are forever gone. On this side of the grave, at least, they are irrecoverable no matter how much genealogical research one might undertake. Their voices have fallen silent; the thought-and-spoken life that had once enlivened their physical bodies was long ago snuffed out with a final breath, leaving only a silent name.

I was reminded of this powerfully when arranging a funeral back when I was a priest in western North Carolina. The deceased, a parishioner's relative I hadn't known personally, had stipulated in her will that all of her diaries were to be cremated with her.

There was something like fifty years' worth of memories locked up in those journals. What they might have told even a casual reader about the deceased's experience of the changes and chances of a life between around 1955 and 2005! Thanks to her will, though, all those recorded memories went up in flames leaving only a mountain of dust for me to pour reverently into a small hole in a patch of earth she never knew. In her case, the return to dust really did amount to a return to silence.

Here then is the first lesson: silence and words bear a close relation to each other. Out of silence come the words that give life and personality. But those words, and thus the life they breathe out, are destined to fall once more into silence. All that can ever endure are recorded words: if not a paradox this is then an irony since the objects giving them permanence – sheets of paper, a cassette tape, a microchip – are flimsier than the bodies that originally produced and contained them. And even here silence pervades; if you've ever read an account of the life of someone you knew, you realize quickly that the real person isn't contained in the facts described but in the silence that lies behind them. Facts only point towards the person, and then only to those who were familiar with him or her.

Yet, there's another way that personalities survive in this world and escape the silent tomb: in the memories of those who survive them. There's a kind of twilit life that endures in the memory of others for a time. I say twilit for two reasons: first, because only flashes of the former life are recalled and, second, because this life quickly becomes fossilized in revision before vanishing entirely.

The flashes are those disjointed moments and conversations that we recall about the person. Often, they're from key moments: a birth, a wedding, times of joy and times of tears. Or they're striking words of advice, anger, praise, humour, love or hatred. These are all more or less memories of real moments but now they've become unmoored, floating free like sparks from a fading fire. The fire that was their life remains only in flashes of memories people later recall and share with others. This is how we know our great-grandparents and the distant relations we've never met but who are alive to us in the few stories about them that have been repeatedly retold.

And then there's the revision. In my ministry to the families of the deceased, I'm often struck by how quickly this editing begins. People rightly don't wish to speak ill of the dead and so almost immediately start highlighting their virtues. Sinners becomes saints in funeral eulogies: two-dimensional in their presentation and transformed into fictional characters by what's left unsaid. There are also harder encounters when the recollected life is composed only of pain, anger and abuse. Once I visited a widow and her grown children in their cramped council house in Oxfordshire to arrange a funeral. When I asked them to recall some memories about the deceased that I might include in my sermon, the widow, with a cold stare, replied: 'There's nothing much about him worth remembering.' The look she and her children gave me spoke far more loudly in their silent intent than any words could.

In the vast majority of cases, even these twilit lives fade within a generation. 'We have but a short time to live. Like a flower we blossom and then wither; like a shadow we flee and never stay.'[1] In a real sense, we're all destined for a double death: the first comes when we no longer draw breath and the second, when all memory of us is forgotten. In the first, we submit entirely to the words of those who survive us. We continue to live in this world only through their stories and in the small influence we had upon them (for good or ill). The subsequent death comes when we're utterly forgotten except by those who may stop to read our epitaphs or who are given to worshipping the dead through their genealogical research.

This is the place in which
the living live in the absence
of all who once were here,
their stories kept a while
in memories soon to be gone
the way of the untongued stories
preceding ours, reduced
to graves mostly lost
and a few found strayed
artifacts of stone.[2]

[1]Church of England, *Common Worship: Pastoral Services* (London: Church House, 2000), 268.
[2]Wendell Berry, 'What Passes, What Remains', in Wendell Berry, *The Art of Loading Brush: New Agrarian Writings* (Berkeley: Counterpoint, 2019), 260.

This is perhaps the great shared horror of humankind: that we live in the face of an oblivion that in the twinkling of an eye erases the experiences, triumphs, tragedies, groped-for insights and hard-earned virtues of a lifetime. If one doesn't believe in life after death, then one must accept that all our rich stories are destined to be silenced forever. The most we can achieve is that we may be well thought of during the brief span of time when we're remembered.

Yet, in many cultures there's another way in which the dead continue to live in the present: tradition. The individual dead are given up to the immense silence of the greater fellowship of their ghostly ancestors and in their company continue to speak to the living. By honouring the dead and appreciating the ideas, beliefs, customs and dreams they collectively held, the dead are allowed to speak. This is, in part, a recognition that all we are now has necessarily emerged from who they were then. Even the mightiest trees must suck nourishment from roots planted deeply and firmly in the soil of dead things. Likewise, even we in the West who don't much honour the dead or give them much thought draw our lives from those who have gone before us. In fact, they've bequeathed to us the very words we speak – except for the neologisms we cobble together from old words like Frankenstein monsters.

Perhaps then, this is the second lesson: the silent dead do continue to speak through the words, ideas, stories and beliefs we inherit from them. We're the continuing conversation of those who've passed over into silence. Their own voices may have ceased, but their words collectively remain to teach if we're disposed to listen or to taunt if we're not. And if we find their words distasteful or even morally repugnant, we still can't entirely escape them because they have been inscribed into our cultural memory. My homeland, the South, exemplifies this: we never seem quite able to silence the voices of our slaveholding past, even when migration from the North and consumer culture have refashioned the South beyond recognition. Likewise, a secular and secularizing Britain remains haunted by its Christian past to the despair of secular triumphalists. Even when we turn our backs on our ancestors and try to block our ears, their words follow us; the present can never truly escape the past no matter how much we like to pretend otherwise.

-oOo-

But I speak as a fool. My sentiments are those of a modern, of someone who, even if his ears are attuned to the voices of the dead, has lived much of his life in flattened landscapes and among people estranged from their forebears. The futility of life – the seemingly incontrovertible fact that lives lived nobly are destined to share the same earthen bed as lives utterly wasted – is for the most part only a preoccupation of us moderns (with the notable exception of *Ecclesiastes*). Our obsession with that futility is what lies behind our collective nihilism: our conviction that existence holds no enduring meaning. How can life be meaningful if its permanence bears no relation to how it's lived? 'Eat and drink for tomorrow we may die' becomes the obvious answer, especially if we aren't taught to see how our own stories were bequeathed by those who preceded us and should yield contentedly to those who'll succeed us. Live your own story to the fullest before the covers are slammed shut for good. 'Just go for it' becomes the mantra of our age. We yearn not so much to enjoy a contented life as to suck it dry before we've blown our chance.

I'm not yet speaking of heavenly matters. I don't think one has to believe in an afterlife in order to find meaning in the world, to see how one's life might escape the silent futility of death. But I do think it's easier to give way to cultural despair when one has already been detached from enduring storied-places: those local landscapes where we can share the company of both the quick and the dead, even if the companionship of the latter is silent. In fact, modernity had to uproot us first in order to convince us that life has little or no meaning beyond, perhaps, how we can add to our nation's GDP by producing and consuming. It really wasn't until masses of people were crammed into cities to eke out lives in industrial production or in front of televisions that we started to be overcome by the silent darkness that awaits us all. Now we rage against the dying of the light by demanding all we can of this life – this rage isn't an act of nobility, like heroes bravely facing death at the hands of their enemies, but one of desperation.

This is where, I think, we begin to see how the paradox of silence and words intersects with the paradox of time and eternity. When our own lives are rooted within a living tradition that's at home in a particular place, then meaning doesn't have to be sought or created. We inherit it from our forebears and naturally pass it on to our heirs. Our personal stories emerge from a long, social conversation, become part of it and are eventually taken up into it through the shared memories and devotion of those we leave behind. The glue here is love: the natural affection for our grandparents, parents, our children and grandchildren.

In his essay 'The Work of Local Culture', Wendell Berry suggests that the modern habit of forgetting – a kind of cultural amnesia that infects our society – is one of the most telling signs of the decay of such love:

> As the exposed and disregarded soil departs with the rains, so local knowledge and local memory move away to the cities or are forgotten under the influence of homogenized salestalk, entertainment, and education. The loss of local knowledge and local memory – that is, of local culture – has been ignored, or written off as one of the cheaper 'prices of progress', or made the business of folklorists . . . when a community loses its memory, its members no longer know one another. How can they know one another if they have forgotten or have never learned one another's stories? If they do not know one another's stories, how can they know whether or not to trust one another?[3]

He recalls the days before television when neighbours would gather at each other's homes, especially during the long nights of winter, to tell and retell stories. In this way, the old and young informed each other's lives, interlocking their stories in a social web that spanned generations.

Moreover, because the young generally didn't move away from home when they became adults, the process of making and sharing stories never ended. Berry imagines this process of memory-making in old farming communities stretching back to the first farmers themselves. That's the authentic kind of tradition that fills the silent selves of individuals to the brim with meaning – with their own place and their own people – and weds them to the land.

> The loss of local culture is, in part, a practical loss and an economic one. For one thing, such a culture contains, and

---

[3]Wendell Berry, 'The Work of Local Culture', in *The World-Ending Fire*, ed. Paul Kingsnorth (London: Penguin, 2017), 107.

conveys to succeeding generations, the history of the use of the place and the knowledge of how the place may be lived in and used. For another, the pattern of reminding implies affection for the place and respect for it, and so, finally, the local culture will carry how the place may be well and lovingly used, and also the implicit command to use it only well and lovingly.[4]

The history of the last hundred years suggests that modernity invariably destroys enduring local cultures, thereby erasing the stories and words of our ancestors. We live amid the great silencing of the past, the disenfranchisement of the dead. The only voices we wish to hear are those of the perpetually young – the would-be Peter Pans who promise to whisk us away to the Neverland of tomorrow. As Berry ominously contends repeatedly in his writings, this imagined land of the future usually paves the way for the destruction of the past and the exploitation of the present. Without the paradox of eternity and time, our quickening paradox of words and silence soon decays.

-o0o-

By far and away my favourite item in Brecon Cathedral is an early twelfth-century font that's covered in elaborate carvings of a jolly-looking green man, animals and spreading foliage. Many people think it's Celtic, but it isn't even Welsh, having been built by Norman craftsmen not long after their arrival here in old Brycheiniog. Like the Cathedral itself, therefore, it's a product of conquest, though (again like the Cathedral) it would have been received by the conquered as a means of life. It's a beautiful piece of medieval artistry, far more elaborate than its younger cousin that I'd seen in the church in Llanfihangel-y-pennant. But its provenance only partly explains why it's my favourite object.

It's still in use – that's the thing that astonishes me. Whenever I conduct a baptism, I pour water from its lead-lined basin over the head of the person (usually a little squawking baby) being welcomed into the Body of Christ. Just think of the countless priests christening countless babies and men and women at that

---

[4]Ibid., 115.

font over the last nearly thousand years. Is there another object like an ancient font that can boast of such enduring employment? Many of the people whose names appear in memorials on the cathedral wall and in its floor were christened in that font – the beginning and end of their lives connected by cathedral stone. Nothing else in Brecon better ties the present to generations past, though the link is only tenuously sustained by the few who are christened nowadays.

This ornate font perfectly expresses the relationship between our own words and silence on the one hand, and timelessness and thick-history on the other. To it are brought the individual stories of those being baptized; in it those stories are plunged into the thick-history of Brecon that stretches back through the ages to the founding generations of this town; from it have come all the movers and shakers, the lowly and downtrodden, the successes and failures, and the heroes and scoundrels who have been Breconfolk since its foundation in the fraught decades following the Norman Conquest.

Most importantly, though, through the water contained in that ancient font, the stories of those silent people have been gathered up into God's own silence and words and are given eternal life. Through baptism and by faith, their stories never returned to silence, grafted as they still are onto the eternal Word from which they arose. I believe they were perfected, too: edited and revised by Christ so that no matter the pain, no matter the tears, no matter the failures those stories contain, they now end in redemption. And redemption, by its very nature, changes how we understand and judge all that preceded it.

Genesis tells us that in the primordial silence of creation, the Spirit moved over the waters. So too, in the silence of baptismal water – and what's more silent than still water? – we receive God's Spirit and the outpouring of God's love. The Spirit of love then interweaves into our own words and silence, giving meaning to our life stories and opening our inner silence up towards God. That Spirit stills the noise of our confused and selfish selves and initiates us into the eternal joy that William of St-Thierry called the 'silence of heaven'. Among the most important words we can ever speak are 'I baptize you in the name of the Father, and of the Son, and of the Holy Spirit.'

Through the waters of baptism and its words of rebirth and renewal, the cries of our silent selves are answered by the Word of our silent God. In that ancient sacrament, the eternal is communicated to us so that our own silence is filled with the Word who is Love. I have seen many a time when something hidden, something silent in a man or woman, bursts out into the open after receiving this silent sacrament and its reassuring words of salvation. In others, baptism has acted more like a seed, planted in the soil of soul and mind, slowly and silently producing its fruit in ways the person hardly recognizes or perceives.

Our old font, therefore, serves a double function. First, as with every font, it's a visible means for and symbol of the new life Christians receive in Christ. A font normally stands near the church entrance, positioned as a sign that through the waters of baptism Christians are brought by faith into the household of God, the Body of Christ. If, as Christians believe, that household transcends time, then we can be assured that the stories told by its members – like a family gathered around a dinner table – will also last, will never fade away into the silence of forgetfulness. At the same time, our particular font by its very age reminds us that this heavenly household isn't removed from our world but penetrates its history, linking one generation to the next. When christenings are conducted as they ought – as a real entry into an actual church rather than just a nice family custom that bears no relation to the church other than conceptually – they behave like Wendell Berry's front porch, drawing the community of the church together generationally and affectionately.

-o0o-

The prophet Ezekiel dreams a mad dream. Four living creatures, bizarre in themselves, bear the faces of the creatures who enjoy dominion on the earth: man over all creatures, eagles over all birds, oxen over all livestock and lions over all wild animals. Here is symbolized all of the natural world standing before the glory of God. It's a wild vision with dust storms, flashes of lightening and an immense ball of fire. After Ezekiel dreams about the four living creatures, he next sees wheels within wheels, like gyroscopes, standing next to each of the creatures: 'When they moved, the others moved; when they stopped, the others stopped; and when they rose from the earth, the wheels rose along with them; for the spirit of the living creatures was in the wheels' (Ezek. 1.21). Beholding this utterly bizarre vision, Ezekiel quite reasonably falls flat on his face.

Like many visions in the Bible, Ezekiel's is mad, lending itself to generations of equally mad interpretations as scholars and preachers have tried to unpack its meaning. The vision has also inspired resonant responses now woven into our own collective imagination. The four living creatures appear again in Revelation before the throne of God, speaking words that now are repeated whenever the Eucharist is celebrated: 'Holy, holy, holy'. Early Christians identified the four faces not with creation itself but with the four Evangelists, Matthew, Mark, Luke and John, which engendered a tradition of iconography that has been shaped in stone, inked on parchment, sewn in ornate fabric and blazoned with colour in stained glass windows. More prosaically, the vision of the wheels has become an evocative way of describing complexity that eludes easy comprehension: wheels within wheels.

Ezekiel's vision provides a useful metaphor for understanding what I began to learn on Cadair Idris. Wheels within wheels describes how the paradoxes relate to each other: the paradox of silence and words revolving around time and eternity. One needs poetry here; it's best suited for showing how silence and time, eternity and silence, time and words, and words and eternity all relate to each other, underpinning, emerging, influencing and responding to each other in ways that delve into the depths of humanity, our selves and creaturely existence. As with the creatures in Ezekiel's vision, somehow our spirit is in those paradoxes.

Just to complicate matters further, there is another wheel in which these two wheels spin – the paradox with which I opened this book, that of heaven and earth, God and humankind. If silence and words are intertwined inextricably with time and eternity, then both are also intertwined with heaven and earth. Silence, words, time and eternity find their respective sources in the God who won't allow them to fall into opposition, who expects even contradictions to be reconciled. We, therefore, have wheels within wheels, complexities upon complexities we can't easily understand or articulate.

We mustn't be surprised, therefore, to find that from the earliest days of Christianity the paradox of silence and words has also been associated with God. For example, during the second century, Ignatius of Antioch, one of the earliest Christian bishops, said that God 'manifested himself through Jesus Christ in his Son, who is his Word that came forth from silence'.[5] Elsewhere, he claims that the

---

[5]Ignatius of Antioch, 'Letter to the Magnesians', in *Early Christian Writing: The Apostolic Fathers*, trans. Maxwell Staniforth (London: Penguin Books, 1968), 8.

Virginity of Mary, the Incarnation and the crucifixion were shouted from the 'deep silence of God'.[6] Silence and words are bound together in a frankly contradictory way with God's own infinite silence shouting the Word that is Christ into our own existence. Yet, Ignatius says, God remains as silent as ever to those lacking the ears, as unnoticed by the world as Jesus was during his earthly ministry.

Ignatius's inspiration must have been the Prologue to John's Gospel: 'In the beginning was the Word, and the Word was with God, and the Word was God.' That magnificent opening places God the Son at the heart of all words, stories and meaning. The Greek word *logos*, translated as 'word', is notoriously difficult to translate – it means something like word, reason, intelligibility, understanding. In Greek philosophy, it referred to the knowing by which we know, the reason by which we reason and the understanding by which we understand; it was thought by Stoics to be the animating principle of the cosmos. At its root, *logos* refers to that which is spoken, and so we're presented again with our paradox: the *logos* is spoken and yet can't be heard by ordinary ears. It's spoken in silence and yet lies behind all words and intelligibility.

'The word is spoken eternally,' wrote Augustine before adding, 'you do not cause it [any creature] to exist other than by speaking.'[7] The Word of God was quickly associated with Genesis 1 where God speaks each day of creation into existence. And yet when that Word came into the world, the 'world knew him not'. John's Gospel prefers the image of light and darkness to silence and words, but the intent is the same: the world that human beings have created is such that it was deaf to the Word when he was uttered into our reality as a human being. The Word 'became flesh and dwelt among us', but the world heard only silence like people who can't hear the soft sounds of nature behind the white noise of human activity.

Here we find early expressions of Divine Silence and the Word that are intimately tied together. The Word is 'shouted' from the silence of God. The Word stands behind all our words, yet does so silently. The Word behind all words even entered our own existence, yet much of humanity couldn't hear him. The Incarnation and our Christian faith may be about speech and proclamation but never about noise. In

---

[6]Ignatius of Antioch, 'Letter to the Ephesians', Ibid., 19.
[7]Augustine, *Confessions*, 11.7.9.

the 'still small voice' of God we encounter both deep silence and the Word that generates all our own stories, both personal and shared.

God's Word and silence bear a close relationship to our own words and silence. We've already seen how our inner selfs would remain silent if we weren't able to communicate it to an external world. Indeed, our inner silence doesn't feel to us like silence because it's filled with words that form our thoughts. That silence is also filled with the remembered words of others that we so absorb over time that we mistake them for our own (to both our benefit and harm); Augustine notes somewhere that through words we indwell each other – we ingest each other's thoughts when we speak and listen and so come to dwell in each other's minds. Every time we chat with others or read their writings, we potentially welcome them to touch our deepest selves and to shape us in ways we may not even perceive.

These thoughts and words enable us to make sense of our silent selves, to strive towards an understanding of who we are and how we should respond to our life experiences. And if the Word of God makes those thoughts meaningful and intelligible, then we can't even begin to know ourselves except through him. He is present in our own thoughts – present, too, in the words and thoughts we share with one another. There's no way for us to be exterior to God, to stand at a distance from him like scientists from their subjects, because he holds our very thoughts, ideas and reasoning together. You might even say that this means that good stories, insofar as they're coherent, meaningful and rational, are God-breathed.

Similarly, God's silence is communicated to us through his Word. Through baptism and by faith, the Word calls the silence of ourselves into the silence of God. St John of the Cross articulated this idea when he wrote, 'The Father spoke one Word, which was his Son, and this Word he speaks always in eternal silence, and in silence must be heard by the soul' and 'Our greatest need is to be silent before the great God . . . for the only language he hears is the silent language of love.'[8] St John reminds us here that God's Word, and the words of our deepest selves, operate at a different level from our normal words: a level that's best described as love. The silent language of love, as anyone who has experienced deep love knows, is far more eloquent than any words can articulate. Divine love, therefore, is the eloquent utterance of God: received in silence but speaking to the very depths of our souls.

If the path to God lies somewhere amid timelessness, thick time and silence, then we're transported up that path by the stories that precede, surround, follow, *are* us. The unchanging, transcendent God who dwells intimately in our thick time calls out to us from his own divine silence through Christ his Word whom we encounter through stories. The tapestry of Scripture, hymns, half-remembered sermons, accounts of faithful men and women and our own personal and family stories makes timelessness and thick time familiar and deep silence less threatening. Perhaps, too, they produce in us a deep yearning to sink more deeply into our existence, to get down beneath the shallows of our everyday lives to encounter a depth we recognize as home. If concepts like eternity and silence seem mystical, our encounter with them through thick time and words means that their mysticism is also earthed or grounded. Heavenly matters come to us wrapped in earthly clothing and, as at our baptism, earthly matter is washed and renewed by heaven. Thus, we discover that heaven is found not only somewhere *out there* but also at the very heart of creation – better still, we find that God is, indeed, all in all.

PART III

The paradox of wonder and the commonplace

FIGURE 3 *Looking west towards Penygadair with the Irish Sea in the distance.*

There I saw Moses blessing the Lord for the precious things of
Heaven, for the dew and for the deep that coucheth beneath:
and for the precious fruits brought forth by the Sun, and for the
precious things put forth by the moon: and for the chief things of
the ancient mountains, and for the precious things of the lasting
hills; and for the precious things of the earth, and fulness thereof.
There I saw Jacob with awful apprehensions admiring the glory of
the world, when awaking out of his dream, he said, How dreadful
is this place. This is none other than the House of God, and the
Gate of Heaven.

THOMAS TRAHERNE, *The Centuries,* III.67.

8

Penygadair

The wonderful

I'm pleased to say I never heard Gwyn ap Nudd's hounds, but neither did I wake up a poet on the following morning (I'll let others comment on the state of my mental health). In the middle of the night, I had been awakened by a team of walkers edging their way widdershins around Llyn Cau and then ascending in pitch darkness up the steep, scree slope that provides a short but precipitous route to the top. For a time, I watched their head torches bob upwards and wondered whether Idris had struck them mad. The next morning, I sat studying their route as I drank my coffee, admiring the shape of the scree, which fans out towards the lake like a shower of gigantic grains of sand stuck in a moment of time. I briefly considered ascending it myself but then shook my head, muttered something about insanity and turned back to my tent to find breakfast. I would leave that climb for another visit.

After my usual trekking breakfast of porridge with brown sugar and cinnamon and another cup of coffee, I broke down my tent, packed up my bag and rejoined the Minffordd Path to begin my climb up to Penygadair, the summit of Cadair Idris. My destination was barely visible as I left my bivouac, looming high above in the gloom of the early morning. The path would take me past Craig Lwyd along the rim of Cwm Cau, leading me clockwise to the summit with the promise of outstanding views along the way. The first morning rays had just appeared above low-lying clouds, bathing the landscape in a pinkish hue. The air was fresh, and a light breeze had begun to rise. It looked like a beautiful day lay ahead.

I passed the spot where I'd watched the setting sun the previous night and continued up the steep slope. As I worked my way around the southern edge of the bowl, I enjoyed continuous views of the lake Tal-y-llyn down in the Dysynni Valley and across to the adjacent mountains. Beneath my feet, the path wound around boulders and took me over weathered rocks and deep gullies where rain and foot traffic had deeply eroded the earth. Eventually, I reached the trickiest part of the day's climb: traversing a high bank of scree still damp and slippery with the morning dew. Fortunately, I'd thought of bringing my trekking poles and with their help picked my way up the broken rock field without much difficulty. At the top, I was afforded an astonishing view down to Llyn Cau, which at that very moment was transformed into a pristine mirror that darkly reflected the early morning's fiery rays. No wonder Cadair Idris is deemed to be a place of enchantment.

As I resumed my journey, a bank of low clouds started flowing like a river of smoke over the ridge and down into Cwm Cau. There must have been a cross-current of air above the lake because the mist vanished as it entered the valley. It was like watching water being poured into a bowl without ever reaching its bottom. It was mesmerizing. For a few minutes, I tried to capture the spectacle on my camera without success, but at least this afforded me an opportunity to rest my legs without having to admit to my ego that I was doing so.

As I continued to ascend, the ground became progressively rocky and otherworldly. The fog that was failing to fill Cwm Cau briefly settled in where I was walking, making the looming rocks along the path appear like vague and ominous shapes in the gun-metal grey of the morning. In places, cairns had been erected to point walkers through the crowd of rock towards the broad path that follows the roughly east-west ridge to the summit. I was grateful for their guidance in the stumbling gloom of the dense fog.

Thankfully, as I neared the bothy at the top of Penygadair, the mist lifted, and I was presented with a spectacular view of western Wales. To the south and east, I could see even more hills and mountains than I did on the previous evening. But now to the west, the Irish Sea stretched into the distance until its blue became indiscernible from the sky. Its choppy waves danced like tiny diamonds along a broad blue field broken only by the scattered black dots of boats. Somewhere just over its horizon lay Ireland, the Emerald

Isle – the sea was once the superhighway of the surrounding Celtic kingdoms, providing water-lanes for saints, traders and invaders. Closer to me were sandy beaches and an inlet where the River Mawddach feeds into the sea with the town of Barmouth nestled on its northern shore. To the north, I could just discern Snowdon and the surrounding mountains that I know so well. The view from atop Cadair Idris on a clear day rates among the best.

I stood there drinking in the incredible views and couldn't help but laugh. I find little more freeing than the sense of space that mountaintops afford. The air had freshened in the morning breeze and the temperature had risen enough for me to take off my jacket and walk in the warmth of the sun from Penygadair along the high broad ridge to the cairn atop Mynydd Moel. I stood for a while at the edge of cliffs that plunge from the north side of Cadair taking photographs and admiring the surrounding countryside. For about an hour, I had the mountain to myself (though I later discovered that the bothy was packed with the slumbering team of climbers from the previous evening). I enjoyed the sublime landscape without a drop of self-consciousness. Wonder filled every inch of me as I strolled in happy reverie around the heights, marvelling at the different perspectives each new vista afforded. I was so ridiculously happy that anyone who might have seen me would have assumed Idris had struck me mad.

-o0o-

As I said at the start of this book, people generally go to the trouble of climbing to the top of mountains to experience something wonderful. The promise of marvels is a powerful motivator, an irresistible pull that draws people higher and higher even as every leg muscle shouts 'stop!' I've sat on many mountaintops enthralled by a kind of wonder that nourishes the soul ever afterwards. I can think of a spot in the Appalachians where on a crisp, autumn morning I admired mountains of yellow, gold, red and orange layered upon each other as far as the eye could see; or a height in Iceland above a broad alluvial plain with neon green hills all around me and a high wall of solidified lava field to my right; or an enormous horizontal rock high up on the Mont Blanc massif with alpine peaks surrounding me and a crevasse-lined glacier below. I could go on.

Wonder and mountaintops go together. You'd have to be a corpse or intensely acrophobic not to be deeply moved by them. It's why so many have been considered the abode of the gods or powerful spirits. Summits feel like divine places where wonder is refined to its essence and offered only to those devout enough to ascend to them. In the words of Robert Macfarlane:

> The true blessing of the mountains is not that they provide a challenge or a contest, something to be overcome and dominated (although this is how many people have approached them). It is that they offer something gentler and infinitely more powerful: they make us ready to credit marvels – whether it is the dark swirl which water makes beneath a plate of ice, or the feel of the soft pelts of moss which form on the lee sides of boulders and trees.... Mountains return to us the priceless capacity for wonder which can so insensibly be leached away by modern existence, and they urge us to apply that wonder to our own everyday lives.[1]

There's nothing we can add to such places of wonder. All we can really do is enjoy them for what they are, delighting in our own inconsequence and the chance simply to enjoy a gift we merited only by our willingness to climb. Life doesn't often afford us such godsends: a 'true blessing' of wonder – that's exactly what a mountaintop is.

Perhaps we need places like high summits to recall the power that wonder has over us. It elates and overwhelms us – or rather, the feeling of overwhelming elation and awe is what we call wonder. The word itself originally referred to the object, the thing that astonishes us, as in the Seven Wonders of the World. Later, its definition expanded to include our emotional response to such marvels: the wonder we feel. In both cases, though, it was reserved for the truly remarkable or astounding, which is how it's used, for example, in the King James Bible: phrases like 'Wonderful Counselor' or the 'wonderful works' of God. During the eighteenth and nineteenth centuries, however, the force of *wonderful* was leached away through overuse to mean simply 'extremely good' as

---

[1]Robert Macfarlane, *Mountains of the Mind* (London: Granta Books, 2003), 274.

when we say, 'What a wonderful present!' We've lost the wonder in wonder.

Yet, I think we mean something more than an appreciation of excellence when we speak of a 'sense of wonder'. Here, we retain something of the older meaning. It involves humility and an innocence that allow us to perceive and enjoy the astonishing reality of our world. To lack a sense of wonder is like not having a sense of humour: a character flaw that keeps you from seeing other dimensions of life and its experiences. To wonder is for a moment to return to our earliest childhood; to have a 'sense of wonder' requires a kind of vulnerability that obliges us from time to time to shed our stuffy adulthood and respond to the world as when we were young.

When we were born and began to explore life outside our mother's womb, the world and wonder almost perfectly coincided. Everything was new and every experience taught us something about life. Babies find their mother's smile wonderful, the crooning of songs even by tone-deaf singers delightful and the most mundane things inducements to laughter. Yes, there are undoubtedly plenty of bumps and bruises they encounter that distress and upset them, but that's part of the process of learning about the harsh realities of life – that all isn't, in fact, delightful. Other than that, everything from our mother's milk to the blue sky are wonders for babies to savour. I can remember my infant son transfixed by his own hand, studying it (or so it seemed to me) as an aesthete might study a sculpture. That form of wonder lies beyond us who have grown old.

To varying degrees, we all lose our capacity for wonder as we age; it is, if you will, how we each abandon Eden like Adam and Eve. Once paradise has yielded to thorns and thistles and toil, we become hardened to the enjoyment of innocent marvels. Yet, except in those tragic cases when life for small children is utterly miserable, we all start from a position of wonder. It's our first experience of this world, our original relationship with creation. We have to be taught to respond to the world differently either by life's circumstances or by continually being told to grow up and never be caught playing the fool. Here again we're like Adam and Eve, for our sense of wonder diminishes as our sense of self increases.

But spend time in the company of children, and you'll often get to glimpse Eden again. I can't help but think here of a day spent by a waterfall in North Carolina where my then seven-year-old son

passed a couple of happy hours fixated on tadpoles. I was enjoying
the sun with my nose in a book, paying little heed to the beauty
around me, entirely ignorant of the little creatures for whom each
pool is a cosmos. But not my son. Those tadpoles captivated him.
He sat there watching them or playfully trying to catch them in
the cup of his hands. He kept pouncing on me in the midst of my
reading, drawing me insistently by the hand to one pool or another
to share his delight. But boring old grown-up that I am, I couldn't
enjoy them as he did. I simply didn't have the capacity for the
sustained wonder that he exhibited.

Little is more wonderful to children than tadpoles; I've never
encountered a child who can resist them. For me, though, it was the
sight of lightning bugs on a sultry evening that filled me with delight.
What's more magical than sparks of light floating like fairies in a
darkening wood? For you it's probably something else. But unless
our souls have completely atrophied, we all have memories of when
the world was filled with magic and (in the old sense of the word)
romance. The memory of such childhood wonders continues to feed
us throughout our life, summoning us back to our first innocence
by our imagination or by living vicariously through our children.
The memory of these early experiences can lift our spirits and even
make us feel young again – recalling now the lightning bugs floating
around our yard made me smile. How often I've experienced
childhood wonders through the stories of the elderly, even some
with profound memory issues.

In *Earth in Mind: On Education, Environment, and the Human
Prospect,* David Orr calls wonder 'part of our original equipment at
birth' that's vital for the flourishing of society.[2] He's speaking here
of our innate response to nature, what he terms the 'sheer joy in
the created world'. In other words, our first impulse is to enjoy the
world around us, to delight in the wonders it offers. But Orr warns,
'As our sense of wonder in nature diminishes, so does our sense
of the sacred, our pleasure in the created world, and the impulse
behind a great deal of our thinking.'[3] To have a sense of wonder is
to be truly alive; it's part of what makes us human.

---

[2]David Orr, *Earth in Mind: On Education, Environment, and the Human Prospect*
(Washington, DC: Island Press, 2004), 23.
[3]Ibid., 24.

Arguably no one catches the childish nature of wonder better
than G. K. Chesterton. In one of my favourite passages, he describes
a childlike God:

> A child kicks its legs rhythmically through excess, not absence,
> of life. Because children have abounding vitality, because they
> are in spirit fierce and free, therefore they want things repeated
> and unchanged. They always say, Do it again; and the grown-up
> person does it again until he is nearly dead. For grown-up people
> are not strong enough to exult in monotony.[4]

To wonder, therefore, is to be childlike and perhaps even godlike.
It's to find joy and elation in something other than ourselves, an
intense delight in another for its own sake. It's to be attuned to the
continual freshness of our ancient world.

There's an irony contained in such wonder as well. Children
throw themselves into experiences of wonder through an excess of
life. Their 'fierce and free' spirits are filled with boundless exuberance
– often much to the despair of weary parents – that draws them to
wonders or makes even everyday things wonderful. And they can be
quite ridiculous in their enjoyment because they have no concept of
what it means to play the fool. This is because 'abounding vitality'
isn't the same as self-awareness. To be full of life doesn't mean to
be full of *you*. In fact, it's usually the opposite. Small children still
have the capacity to throw themselves entirely into their world
and unselfconsciously delight in the wonders around them. Their
enjoyment is uninhibited, which makes wonders more *present* and
real. It's an act of the imagination rather than of reason or the will.
Our imagination is so much freer than these.

Chesterton, however, raises a crucial point about wonder: it can't
long endure monotony or even, I would add, familiarity. The initial
magic of a wonder quickly fades. The medieval historian Caroline
Walker Bynum points out that 'only that which is really different
from the knower can trigger wonder',[5] and so familiarity breeds if

---

[4]G. K. Chesterton, *Orthodoxy: The Romance of Faith* (New York: Image Books, 1990), 60.

[5]Caroline Bynum Walker, 'Wonder', *The American Historical Review*, 102:1 (February 1997), 3.

not contempt then boredom, which dispels the enchantment that first held us. I'm continually struck by my own inability to sustain a sense of wonder in the face of familiarity. If I stand atop Pen y Fan in the Brecon Beacons, as I do with some regularity, and take in the majestic views that surround me, the feeling now has nothing like its first intensity. When my hill running takes me past its cairn, normally festooned, with posing day-trippers, I hardly ever remain long to admire the view. Familiarity has leached away some of the peak's majesty. There's no returning to your first kiss.

In his essay 'On Fairy Stories', the fantasy-writer and philologist J. R. R. Tolkien suggests that the opposite of wonder is triteness. Things become dull through overuse or overexposure:

> the things that are trite, or (in a bad sense) familiar, are the things that we have appropriated, legally or mentally. We say we know them. They have become like the things which once attracted us by their glitter, or their colour, or their shape, and we laid hands on them, and then locked them in our hoard, acquired them, and acquiring ceased to look at them.[6]

Our capacity for boredom knows almost no bounds. Seen often enough, even the most spectacular marvels become monotonous. The extraordinary sinks into the mire of ordinariness and soon the grass starts to look far greener on the other side. Then we become restless and either start searching for other wonders to delight us or turn our minds to improving the place that once so enchanted us – often to the detriment of all.

-o0o-

Perhaps our difficulty in sustaining wonder in the face of familiarity lies at the heart of our world's disenchantment. The German philosopher Max Weber was the first to propose that our scientific, bureaucratic and rationalied world banishes gods, spirits, and the supernatural from our world. Fairies and spirits may have resisted kings and warriors, but their old magic proved impotent against managers, scientists, and bureaucrats. Our world has become

---

[6]J. R. R. Tolkien, *Tolkien On Fairy-stories, Expanded Edition, with Commentary and Notes*, ed. Verlyn Flieger and Douglas A. Anderson (London: HarperCollins Pub., 2008), 67.

known and managed (though perhaps not with the success we once assumed) and thus less mysterious and wild. With the old gods and spirits have gone also the transcendent ideals that bind us together and enable us to find meaning and wholeness communally. Instead, we must now seek fulfilment on our own, like intrepid explorers of old, armed mainly with the tools of science, psychology and technology – fine perhaps if we manage to stumble upon El Dorado, but just as likely to end with us lost in the jungle of modern life. A disenchanted world is often a lonesome one.

I'm not saying that one can't be a scientist and feel wonder. Wonder is where science starts. It's the child who marvels at the stars who becomes an astronomer or the one who plays with tadpoles that becomes a biologist. Without wonder, there would be no curiosity, as we see again in children. The marvels of the world draw us towards themselves, inviting us to strive towards better appreciation and understanding. At its best, science is simply the meeting of wonder and knowledge for the benefit of others.

All the same, we tend to prize rational inquiry and understanding above a sense of wonder – the former is *useful* while the latter is merely an enjoyable state of mind. It may be pleasant to feel wonder, but it doesn't really achieve much of anything – that is, of course, except happiness. There's no way to measure it either. We have developed efficient means for testing the soundness of reason and quantifying knowledge but lack the means for doing the same with a sense of wonder. Nor do we really want to. A strong sense of wonder, after all, complicates many of our modern strivings: people who delight in a landscape are unlikely to turn its forests and fields into housing estates or build a chemical plant along its clear river waters. In terms of our social and economic policies, we prefer the world to be more knowable and useful than wonderful.

In fact, ambivalence about wonder has been part of the push of progress from the dawn of modernity. The philosopher René Descartes believed that while wonder is our first passion and useful for inspiring us to discover new things, it also 'can entirely block or pervert the use of reason'.[7] He therefore concluded that our sense of wonder needs moderation through reflection, attentiveness and examination. In philosophical terms, he was telling everybody

[7]René Descartes, *Passions of the Soul*, ar. 76, trans. Stephen Voss (Indianapolis: Hackett Publishing Co., 1989), 59.

to grow up. We see this sentiment repeated like a mantra by the successors of Descartes: wonder is a good and necessary place to begin but don't linger there long if you wish to become enlightened. To progress, childish wonder must yield to adult inquiry and examination for new knowledge and understanding to arise. Knowledge always trumps wonder and mystery; all things must be knowable so that they can be appropriated for the betterment of humankind.

But if we think of wonder and enchantment as intricately linked, I think we can better understand why we need to keep and nurture a sense of wonder. In literature, enchanted items and places are either sacrosanct or threatening (or both). A child would undoubtedly find it odd for an enchanted forest to be logged in a fairy tale (unless by villains), and no one ever suggested that Excalibur should be studied, replicated and mass-produced for King Arthur's knights. Rather, the appropriate attitude towards enchantment and marvels is reverence, even deference. Such wonders lie beyond human tinkering and influence, preserved from our normal needs and desires, and never treated lightly. Folktales are full of cautionary tales of fools who failed to respect this ancient law to their own cost or demise. Our current climate crisis and ecological calamities suggest that this is a lesson we must relearn.

Wonder and enchantment insist that we accept that we're not the world's masters, that much must remain outside our reach and beyond our insatiable desire to tinker and mould for our own use. They dispose us towards accepting our own subjectivity and our creaturely vulnerability to an immensely larger and more enigmatic world than we can ever comprehend or master. Indeed, a belief in the value of wonder involves more than grudging acceptance but, rather, finds contentment and even joy in the mystery of reality. Our reverence for the wonder of creation also involves the willingness to accept a middling status – 'made little lower than the angels' (Ps. 8.5) – rather than toiling endlessly to become gods, masters of every atom of creation. By refusing to be divine, we gladly accept our creatureliness – our place within the community of creation rather than outside it. We allow the rest of creation to enjoy its own worth apart from us.

This takes us once again to the connection between wonder and childlike innocence. Children don't need to be told that much in this world lies beyond their control; unsuccessful temper tantrums and scrapes and bruises teach them soon enough. But they also have what the great compiler of fairy tales Andrew Lang called an 'appetite for marvels', which demands only that wonders remain wonderful. They have no need for someone to explain how Excalibur is stuck in a stone in such a way that only the rightful king of Britain can free it or why Sleeping Beauty will remain asleep until Prince Charming is overcome by her beauty. We adults may need to explain or even revise these stories (tied as they sometimes are to discarded sentiments), but children accept them like they do many things in their world: simply as marvels. They have an innate sense of their appropriateness within the stories being told.

Even in our disenchanted age, though, we do in some ways retain a similar respect for wonder, though often not without some resistance. John Muir, the great conservationist, was so overcome by the wonders of Yosemite that he campaigned hard to have it designated a national park, our modern method for classifying certain places as worthy of special reverence. To cross the boundary into a national park or nature preserve, like old sacred groves or enchanted mountains, is to leave our everyday world for an exceptional one. We happily mark such places from the rest of world, designating them forever free from human exploitation and, often, permanent habitation. The globe is now dotted with officially designated places of wonder, like Cadair Idris, that have earned their respected status purely on the grounds that they strike us as being particularly wonderful. Violate such places and people get just as angry as in olden days when sacred precincts were desecrated, as can be seen by public reaction to fracking near the Lake District in England or oil exploration in the caribou-rich Arctic north. People who have no intention of ever climbing to Everest Base Camp are deeply upset to learn of the rubbish that's strewn there.

So, we find in wonder a mixture of childlikeness and enchantment. To experience wonder is for a time to return to our first innocence, to experience the world afresh and enjoy its magic once more. A 'sense of wonder', therefore, involves a degree of humility, a willingness to delight in the newness of the world, to be a child again. When I reached the summit of Penygadair, all that was required was for me to be receptive to the wonders that lay all around me. I could exert no control over them, could make no demands of them and certainly could gain no fundamental knowledge from them. But I could remain in their presence and allow them to act upon me in ways beyond my control. By not viewing the wonders as things

needing explanation, I was free to experience them as mysteries
to be savoured. By so doing, I did gain knowledge, only it wasn't
knowledge of the things I was enjoying but, rather, of myself.

In a way, that's precisely what I hope this book exemplifies.

-oOo-

Scholars who turn their attention to the idea of wonder often note
the strong desire it conjures in our hearts. When we're overcome by
a marvellous experience, we yearn to repeat it. When I was thrilled
by the wonder of the Appalachian Mountains during my first long
hike in the Shining Rock Wilderness, I knew for certain that I had
to return again and again. That experience awoke within me a
deep passion for the wilderness, a need to amble regularly away
from human habitation and stand for a time in the great theatre
of nature. Other wonders have since fed that hunger without ever
satisfying it; indeed, it has now become part of who I am.

This is to say that the impact of wonder on us is more than a
little like falling in love. We're disarmed by our first encounters with
marvels, swept up by elation and gripped by a strong affection for
them. There's little that is rational about this process; we can't even
tell if a purported wonder will overwhelm us. I've been in places
famous for their beauty and majesty that have left me perhaps not
unaffected but certainly not particularly besotted. On the other
hand, there are places that have touched me so deeply that they're
now never far from my thoughts. I'm regularly drawn unexpectedly
into a reverie about them (usually during a long meeting or a
sermon) that produces in me much the same contentment I feel
when I dream about the people I deeply love like my wife or my son.

But if the elation of wonder is like falling in love, then it would
seem to be a promiscuous love. Familiarity often disrupts the
relationship by cooling the emotions we first felt and encouraging
us to search elsewhere for romance. As with our romantic loves, I
suppose, this is felt more powerfully by some than by others. Many
are happy to relish the wonders around them and simply know and
love them ever more deeply over the years. Often during my morning
walks, I pass a gentleman who has been walking the same paths in
the wood behind Brecon Cathedral for the last twenty years or more.
The same woods, the same trails, the same babbling river (though
with successive dogs), yet he's as happy with them as ever. The global

tourist industry would suggest, however, that most of us aren't like that. We're more like philanderers who measure love by quantity rather than quality. We suck one wonder dry of its emotional impact before moving onto the next or, worse, stay for only a brief tryst that we record on our camera phones to share on social media. My own catalogue of such photos fills several gigs on my hard drive.

It's easy to be dismissive of such encounters. Tourism bears a heavy ecological cost and degrades wonderful places as millions swarm to them. The recent Covid-19 lockdown revealed to us the damage such mass tourism inflicts on these locales. But I think even our promiscuous relationships with the world's wonders speak to something vital about us. Like many wanton lovers, people who flit from one wonder to another are searching for something. They recognize a connection between the marvels they visit: a shared feeling, sense or experience that marks them out from all other places. They know that to visit any one is to visit them all. They produce the same effect, cause the same yearning and meet the same need. I think we crave to be transported out of the ordinary into the extraordinary – for a moment to dwell outside of our own world in another that we sense lies all around us even if we can't normally see it. To encounter places of wonder is to experience something akin to entering the wardrobe into Narnia, rising somewhere over the rainbow or taking 'the second star to the right, and straight on till morning'.

Perhaps no one expresses this yearning better than C. S. Lewis. A major theme of *Surprised by Joy*, his autobiographical account of his road to conversion, is his regular encounters with *otherness*, a feeling of something lying just beyond his vision that evoked in him a deep yet mysterious desire. 'It was something quite different from ordinary life and even from ordinary pleasure,' he recalls of an early experience of this wonder, 'something, as they would now say, "in another dimension"'.[8] He names that dimension 'Joy' and shows how his longing for it led him from rationalism and atheism back to the Christian faith. But, against the expectations of the reader, that process also led him to realize that his encounter with Joy wasn't the goal or object of his longing but only a sign pointing towards

---

[8]C. S. Lewis, *Surprised by Joy: The Shape of My Early Years* (San Diego: Harcourt Brace & Company, 1955), 17.

it, 'not the wave but the wave's imprint on the sand'.[9] The object,
Lewis claims, is God.

In the same way, our encounters with wonder point us towards
something else. The innocence and humility they require or awaken
within us are *billets des passage* that allow us momentarily to
escape our everyday world, to glimpse something which our hearts
have long desired.

> One thing I asked of the Lord,
>   that will I seek after:
> to live in the house of the Lord
>   all the days of my life,
> to behold the beauty of the Lord. (Ps. 26.4)

We know that these moments can't last – we can't remain on
mountaintops forever and must surely descend back to the valleys
of our everyday lives. But we also know that a world without such
mystical wonders would be a poorer one. I believe this sense of
otherness – let's call it transcendence – is fundamental to human
flourishing. It's the seedbed for our imagination, the humus from
which love grows, the rich loam for producing hope. Those who
know best where that other world may be found amid our own
world, who recognize the immeasurable value of wonder, are also
those who know how best to live in this world. It's in the very
nature of wonder to enchant.

-oOo-

Wonder is perhaps the one essential ingredient for the religious
frame of mind. Without it there can be no faith, no yearning for
God, no dissatisfaction with this fallen world. Without wonder
there's not even a sense of the divine, which may explain why a
disenchanted world is often also a godless one. Only in a world
charged with grandeur can we discover or even conceive of the
sacred, of a beauty that leaves us breathless with awe and convinced
of some transcendent *other*. And that wonder requires hearts with
enough residual youth to be filled with delight. David Orr suggests

[9]Ibid., 219.

that a sense of wonder is fragile and, once lost, is only regained with difficulty.[10] Perhaps when Jesus taught his disciples about the need to be like little children, what he meant was that they needed to regain their sense of wonder.

Once, all this was instinctive. The people who erected Stonehenge or constructed the Parthenon above Athens or imbued basilicas with Gothic light and ornamentation understood the connection between wonder and the sacred. But such was the antipathy towards wonder during the great Enlightenment project that divine wonder was devalued not only in the world but also in our churches. Instead, we embraced the rational principles they believed modern man required for fashioning a better world. The connection between wonder and the divine was broken – worse still, wonder was enlisted to magnify western man. Finding our own ingenuity wonderful, we neglected to see the marvels that point away from us and towards God.

Even when there was a reaction to that sentiment during the nineteenth-century romantic movement, wonder returned mainly to our aesthetic world, as we see in the Neo-gothic and restored medieval churches that epitomize Victorian notions of beauty. Though many worked hard to reintroduce wonder to our worship, prayers and spiritual life, they never quite succeeded. Man was too much in the ascendency; and little was less childlike than the self-confident men (and they were mainly men) of high modernity. Enchanting wonder was largely exiled to children's literature, which not coincidentally began to flourish: everything from *The Secret Garden* and *Alice in Wonderland* to *The Hobbit* and *Narnia*.

That only tells us again that a sense of wonder requires humility. We must be made to feel small before we can begin to wonder. Children are naturally small and powerless, and so wonders appear easily and naturally to them. We, on the other hand, are often too full of ourselves, too confident in our own knowledge, and too sure of our own understanding to embrace readily a sense of wonder that feels divine. And a people inured to divine wonder quickly become a people for whom nothing is sacred, nothing taboo, nothing beyond their infernal desire to tinker. Where there's no divine wonder, there's usually only drudgery or wills bent towards rapacity.

---

[10]Orr, *Earth & Mind*, 23–4.

And this, finally, is why the connection between wonder and God is so essential to our own well-being. When wonder is rooted in some sense of the sacred and of things beyond our control or even understanding, it places limits on our constant, hungry, greedy need to meddle. It restrains our overweening belief that we have a right over all things, that our dominion of the earth knows no bounds, is obedient to no higher authority. Without such wonder not only is the planet broken but our humanity is also diminished. We become a scourge, a plague, the ruination of much that is naturally good and flourishing. Perhaps the difference between us and locusts is therefore found as much in our sense of wonder as in genetics; we can't readily destroy and consume that which amazes and astonishes us.

9

Rhiw Gwredydd

The commonplace

After I had spent a good hour lost in the wonder of Penygadair, I reluctantly made my way back down via the Pony Path to Mary Jones's chapel and my car. As I began my descent from Penygadair, below me to my right lay Llyn y Gadair, the largest of three lakes on the northern side of the mountain. I was tempted to visit it, to view Cadair Idris along its northern face, but I didn't have the time or, to be honest, the energy to descend and reclimb the thousand feet. Instead, I left the main path and picked my way along 'The Saddle' in order to extend my enjoyment of the views over the lake. Afterwards I cursed my detour as I stumbled my way down a tiresome field of shattered rock. You often have to work for your wonders.

My view of what lay beyond Cadair Idris became increasingly limited as my elevation dropped. First, many of the mountains to the south sank beneath the horizon of the slopes above me, next Barmouth and the blue waters of the river and then, finally, any glimpse of the Irish Sea. For the most part, they were replaced by endless peat and turf – views not without their own charm but also not so different from what I saw regularly back home. By then, I also no longer had the mountain to myself. Other walkers toiled upwards towards the summit in the late morning sun. A few stopped for a friendly chat, others could only nod as they staggered onwards through a mental stew of exhaustion and determination. For a time, the silence was broken by an unhappy woman loudly berating her man for hauling her up the mountain; the lengthening physical distance between them as she fell farther behind him seemed to reflect their emotional bond. Not everyone enjoys the wonder of mountains.

Eventually, I reached the crossroads in the path and turned left to continue my descent down Rhiw Gwredydd, a narrow valley that falls steeply away towards the Dysynni Valley and shelters a stream that eventually becomes Afon Cadair. Now, my walk became a slow return to regular life. I gradually rejoined the world of human habitation: cultivated and fenced-in farmland turned into scattered farmhouses and finally the lovely little homes that comprise Lanfihangel-y-pennant. Soon, I rejoined the paved road and found myself back among civilization. My escape had come to an end.

I find the transition back into the world of human activity a disconcerting experience. There's part of me that would happily live like a hermit in the wilderness; I think I could even manage without a great many modern amenities. The pace of the natural world fits my own pace better, and I regret the return to the clocks and schedules of my normal life and the confines of offices, meeting rooms, and even a home. Of course, I like having a roof over my head (I'm not that crazy), but I do wish that so much of my life weren't spent indoors and staring at screens.

Part of this dis-ease arises from my inability to resist slipping back into old habits that I don't like but modern life encourages. Out on the mountain, there's no temptation to sit idle for too long or to waste time on social media or watching television. People like to think that life outdoors is somehow simpler, but it isn't – just consider the work that's required to make a cup of coffee or the bother of getting ready for bed in a small tent. Lighting a campfire is far more complex than turning the dial on a thermostat. Life outdoors is simpler only in the more limited range of choices it offers, most of which require or encourage activity. When I go trekking, I find that by the time I've set up my tent, inflated my sleeping mat, unpacked my sleeping bag, finished with dinner and washed up, I'm ready to curl up with a good book and call it a day. When I'm alone, reading and reflecting are really my only two options. How quickly that changes, though, back home where the range of choices seems to encourage idleness and distraction. I suppose I'm the sort of person who is either outdoors and constantly active or indoors and idle. I'm too much like my dogs in that respect.

My long treks in the wilderness prompt a melancholic awareness in me of how different our artificial world is from the natural. I think

I first became aware of this feeling after a retreat at Monck's Corner, a Trappist abbey in South Carolina. I lived with the monks for three days in a haven of contemplative silence, order and tranquillity with nothing to mark the passage of time except the sun, set times for prayer and my own thoughts and reflections. I read an excellent novel, wandered through the abbey's luscious gardens, admiring their live oaks bearded with Spanish moss, or simply sat in silent reverie near the Cooper River. Afterwards, my return to our world of commonplace consumerism came as a shock to the system – its tacky billboards, heavy traffic, strip malls, fast food joints, all tethered together by sagging electrical and telephone cables seemed offensive. In comparison to the abbey, suburban America felt like a great cancerous sore spreading over the Carolina countryside. The abbey was ordered by God and nature, the outside world for profit. Jesus' warning about the impossibility of serving both God and Mammon seemed manifest in the stark contrast between cloister and conurbation.

The great travel writer, Patrick Leigh Fermor noted a similar experience when he returned to Paris after spending months with the Benedictines at the ancient Abbey of St Wandrille de Fontanelle. He writes:

> If my first days at the Abbey had been a period of depression, the unwinding process, after I had left, was ten times worse. The Abbey was at first a graveyard; the outer world seemed afterwards, by contrast, an inferno of noise and vulgarity entirely populated by bounders . . . and crooks. . . . From the train which took me back to Paris, even the advertisements for Byrrh and Cinzano seen from the window, usually such jubilant emblems of freedom and escape, had acquired the impact of personal insults. The process of adaptation – in reverse – had painfully to begin again.[1]

Fermor was writing in the 1950s when modernity and consumerism were only beginning to transform our landscapes. How much more jarring the experience of return and adaptation is today.

---

[1]Patrick Leigh Fermor, *A Time to Keep Silence* (London: John Murray, 1957), 46–7.

This transition back to the everyday is hardest for me after a long trek. The process of slipping into a slower pace and an idling frame of mind that comes during days on foot is hard to reverse – the sensation is not unlike pulling out from a country road onto a five-lane highway at the height of rush hour. Everything seems too fast-paced and too in-your-face to take in properly. That's exactly the point. Away from human activity, you can be utterly attentive, soaking in everything through your senses because nothing is really happening. Often in our world, everything is happening all at once – there's no way to take it all in, to be attentive to it all, without long-learned mental filters. Those filters fall away when you escape that bedlam for a time. But when you return, you're left feeling strangely autistic until those filters fall back into place. At least I do.

My starkest experience of this came at the end of a nearly three-week trek with my wife in France, from Grenoble to Avignon. We enjoyed glorious sunshine and the peaceful Provençal landscape, walking along empty paths and around fields recently harvested of their lavender. When we at last arrived in Avignon, I found that I needed about a day before I could properly enjoy the architectural beauty of the Palais du Papes, the Cathedral and the other splendid buildings. I was simply too distracted by the crowds of people, the ever-flowing traffic, and the hubbub of city life. During the trek, I'd settled into a more sedate mode and so needed time to readjust to modern life, even amid the beauty of that prosperous medieval city.

To a lesser degree, I felt the same way as I left Cadair Idris. As I turned the ignition on my car and reversed out of my parking space, I felt like a drug addict having to cope with coming down. The highs I'd felt atop Cadair Idris couldn't last for ever. Wonders are by their very nature exceptional: moments and occasions that pop up during the humdrum of our all-too-ordinary lives, only to vanish quickly like the brilliant light of a meteor as it fizzles away into nothing. Looking ahead to my return to a broken marriage, a busy teaching schedule and a college in the process of a radical restructuring, I had even more reasons to rue my journey back into normal life. I also believed that this would be my last trip to the mountains of north Wales for a long time. In three months, I would be moving alone to Oxford to start a new life and role there amid dreamy spires but far away from any mountains.

-oOo-

One of my personal failings is that I'm an explorer rather than a settler. I too blithely blame my nomadic life on circumstances beyond my control. In reality, when life starts to feel ordinary, as my daily routines become established and I find it harder to find new places to explore, part of me wants to up sticks and move to new pastures. I suppose I use the outdoors like others use their television or their laptop. Exploring new landscapes may be healthier than sitting in front of a screen and cheaper than going to gigs, but I'm as hooked on thrills as the most addicted gamer or clubber. I eagerly anticipate the chance to follow untaken paths or admire new vistas like a teenager a new game or album. We're all trying to escape boredom, the banality of so much of our modern life.

Such escapism is as much a feature of our lives as hard work and drudgery were for our ancestors. When wonders are often a keystroke, button or swipe of the credit card away, why settle for anything less? We flee from everyday reality by diving into other worlds, other realities, far more entertaining than anything we encounter in real life. Films, video games, shopping, mobile phones and social media are indispensable tools – we might even say household gods – of our everyday lives. Photos of parents with their faces turned towards their phones rather than their babies have become icons of our age. Paradoxically, escaping the commonplace has become, well, ordinary.

Modernity has made us dissatisfied with everyday life. We've been fed such a steady diet of wonders – our expectations have been so relentlessly raised – that we feel a right to live extraordinary lives or, at least, to have a steady diet of spectacular experiences. Who wants to be ordinary? Who doesn't want to live an amazing life? The commonplace is just another name for dull. We want our lives to be special; we want to be special. An ordinary life seems somehow to be a wasted life. In the film *Dead Poets Society*, Robin Williams's character Mr Keating tells his students, 'Carpe diem. Seize the day, boys. Make your lives extraordinary.' Using all the resources available to us, we gladly heed his advice: carpe diem is the mantra for an age haunted by a pathological aversion to being ordinary.

Our sense of the commonplace, however, isn't stable. Once any wonder becomes common, it can no longer remain wonderful; drained of enchantment, it's reduced to the mundane. In 1910, someone driving around town in an automobile would have been the cause of much fascination and comment; by the 1930s such a scene was common. I can recall the first time I had access to email and being amazed that I was chatting live with strangers in Germany, Britain and Japan from a computer lab at William & Mary in Virginia. How ordinary that experience is now! One could go on almost ad infinitum – the wonders of the twentieth century practically spilled over each other, making the shelf life of any given wonder astonishingly short. Our marvels now are either soon superseded and thus become fads or mass-produced and thus become ordinary. In either case, they no longer hold our fascination.

The same is true of even those wonders that are obvious goods. Not all that long ago, many people in America and Europe didn't enjoy decent medical care. The ability to pop down to the pharmacy to purchase effective pain relievers, antihistamines or cold medicine wasn't common or even possible. Now it has become so ordinary that access to good medical care is upheld as a fundamental human right. We never stop to think, 'Goodness, isn't it amazing that when I'm laid low by a headache, I can just swallow a couple of tablets to ease the pain?' Similarly, real hunger has never been part of my everyday experience, even though it remains all too common in developing countries and among the destitute living among us – really, it's the constant companion and motivator of almost all animal life. How extraordinary then is my ability to eat almost anything I want even in late winter! And yet, because this marvel of industrial agriculture is now commonplace, I take it for granted – it's a part of my ordinary life.

Medical care and cheap food are only two examples of how ordinary life in the affluent West remains extraordinary to most people on our planet. We take for granted a whole range of comforts and securities that the vast majority of people rarely if ever enjoy – warmth, security, food, clean water, health care, comfort and personal freedom have neither been nor are the common lot of men and women. We know this, and yet our sense of the commonplace is still greedy, even miserly – no blessing can satisfy our desire to be extraordinary once that blessing becomes widely shared. This fact lies near the heart of our growing inequalities since the pursuit of the spectacular almost invariably depends on leisure and wealth.

When the world appeared to be an infinite source of potential wonders, perhaps this relentless pursuit of new wonders was permissible. As long as you helped or didn't obstruct others from pursuing their dreams, experiencing (according to their own definition) a good life that escapes the tedium of ordinary life, then you could seize the day for yourself without much guilt. The development of our notion of 'lifestyles' is the fruit of this mindset. We now take it as normal and morally defensible to spend vast sums of money accessorizing our lives. Self-expression is another way of saying that we're art – and if so, then we must display ourselves in eye-catching ways. How many of our so-called friends on social media are, in fact, primarily *images* that flit attractively across our screens (profile photos, holiday snaps, selfies, etc.), more like the moving portraits in *Harry Potter* than flesh-and-blood human beings?

The American philosopher Richard Rorty termed this the 'aesthetic life', in which people pursue 'self-enlargement' or 'self-enrichment' in order to satisfy their desire 'to embrace more and more possibilities, to be constantly learning, to give oneself over entirely to curiosity'.[2] We draw on all the resources available to us to enrich our lives as much as possible; this is the basic impulse now in the West and what defines our aspirations. The pragmatist philosopher Richard Shusterman notes:

> It is demonstrated by our culture's preoccupation with glamour and gratification, with personal appearance and enrichment. The celebrated figures of our time are not men of valour or women of virtue but those significantly called the 'beautiful people'. We are less inclined to the imitation of Christ than to imitate the cosmetics and fashions of Princess Diana; no one today reads the lives of saints for edification and example, but the biographies of film stars and the success stories of corporate millionaires are perennial best sellers.[3]

We've become the collectors of spectacles, wonders and experiences in our desperate bid to be extraordinary or, at least, to be seen by others to be enjoying extraordinary lives.

Comparing our lives with those of the wealthy, beautiful and famous is to embrace a fiction, to measure ourselves against *images* of happiness that reinforce ideals built on the shifting sands of fantasy.

---

[2]Richard Rorty, 'Freud and Moral Reflection', in *Essays on Heidegger and Others: Philosophical Papers* (Cambridge: Cambridge University Press, 1991), 154.
[3]Richard Shusterman, 'Postmodern Aestheticism: A New Moral Philosophy?', *Theory, Culture & Society*, 5 (1988): 337–8.

I'm solidly middle class by British standards. That makes me wealthier than 96 per cent of the people living on the planet. Put bluntly, my own life is more similar to a billionaire's than to almost everyone else alive. Sure, I understand this at some notional level and feel a twinge of unease, yet, ultimately, not enough to sacrifice my standard of living substantially to improve the ordinary lives of others. We're adept at expressing sympathy for the downtrodden while remaining motivated by the powerful and successful. I wonder what God makes of me, a priest who daily offers prayers for the downtrodden while living like a lord. I'm too much like the rich man in Jesus' parable, feasting sumptuously amid a whole host of Lazaruses.

When we start to view our lives as *objets d'art*, the commonplace becomes synonymous with the unremarkable: the standard against which we measure our ambition. In our drive to better ourselves, improve our lives and make people notice us amid the great sea of humanity, we *must* become extraordinary people. We work harder, gain more qualifications, earn more money, pursue fame, glory or even notoriety, and are even reduced to collecting 'likes' and 'friends' on social media like dragons their treasure-hoards. There's almost nothing we won't do to be seen as somehow special, to show that at least something in our lives isn't common.

This way of living doesn't come cheaply. If we expect our neighbours to be anything other than ordinary – say, perhaps by constantly demanding that they pay attention to us, or cater to our needs, or conform to our beliefs and sensitivities – then we'll constantly be disappointed, outraged and angry. If we expect our relationships to soar to the heights of Hollywood then our friends, families and lovers will never satisfy us. If we prefer the fictitious or far-flung folk on our screens to the actual men, women and children who live around us, then our local communities will continue to decline as we fall prey to isolation and resentment. If we expect life to always entertain and thrill us, then we'll suck it dry of its capacity to do anything but bore and disappoint us as we wear ourselves out in the process.

The final problem with the aesthetic life is its unsustainability. The climate crisis is a stark reminder that God didn't create the world to be a magical box of treats into which we can blithely dip to retrieve anything we want to make our lives extraordinary. The wonders we in the West have made common have wrought astonishing destruction in a disturbingly short period of time. We've toxified our waterways, destroyed our soil, spread plastic around the globe, raised mountains of rubbish and instigated the Anthropocene. It's quickly become apparent that our own exaggerated sense of the commonplace and insatiable desire to transcend it may leave behind an impoverished and ruined planet for our children and grandchildren. The climate crisis is a horrifying judgement on our cherished conviction that progress comes cost-free.

Ultimately, however, our sense of what we can and should expect from life arises not from apocalyptic visions of the future but from our experience of everyday life compared with those around us. If what we are, do, consume and achieve doesn't stand out positively from those around us, then we're just commonplace, run-of-the-mill, nothing to write home about. If what we are, do, consume and achieve is less than what's commonplace among those around us, then we're among the pitied, the cast-offs, the lazy. Either way, the people we yearn to call our own are those more affluent, better looking, happier or more famous than we are. At the moment, we're just clicking our ruby slippers and hoping that we can continue our magical lives in a sustainable fashion.

-o0o-

Between writing that last line and this one, I conducted a funeral for a local gentleman who lived to the ripe old age of eighty-seven. He had spent his entire life in Brecon and in the course of his life had been a Cathedral chorister, husband, father, insurance salesman, and a rugby coach. As I listened to his family recount stories about his life and, later, to his eulogy tearfully read during the funeral, I could point to almost nothing that I hadn't heard a hundred times. Although his life was enormously special to those who mourned him, from an aesthetic point of view it was utterly unremarkable – his eulogy might have been summed up thus: 'He was an ordinary man, who lived an ordinary life in an ordinary town.'

After his burial on a hillside on a cold afternoon in almost horizontal rain, I reflected on other funerals I've conducted over the years. My ministry to the recently bereaved has been rewarded by the biographies I've encountered in lives lovingly remembered. There's tremendous wisdom to be gained in listening to people recollect the lives of those they've lost. Collectively, they express the commonplace experience of living, loving and being loved.

138 A PILGRIMAGE OF PARADOXES

Often careers are only briefly mentioned in family eulogies, which invariably focus on the ordinary components of domestic love. Of greater worth is the extraordinary mother or husband than the successful worker. I often wonder how different these eulogies would be if the deceased had composed them. Usually what we value turns out to be fool's gold and what we take for granted is precisely what people most love about us.

Funerals have taught me that even though we may want to escape the ordinary, pulling ourselves (if need be) out of the commonplace reality of modern life, it's actually in *that* reality that we grow and are shaped. There's a great myth believed by many affluent people that wonderful experiences change us and expand our horizons. But that's usually a lie, something we tell ourselves perhaps to excuse lavish holidays and expensive experiences. Ordinarily, we consume these adventures like we do new TV shows or gadgets, easily enjoying their thrills but just as easily discarding them once they're over or can no longer hold our attention. What really makes us who we are is the ordinary experience of our commonplace lives.

The trick, though, is to learn to appreciate our own ordinariness, to find meaning not in striving to make our lives extraordinary but in the stability of living well among the ordinary people around us. Here, we have Jesus as our ideal. Paul commends Jesus' ordinariness for us to emulate: 'Let the same mind be in you that was in Christ Jesus, who, though he was in the form of God, did not regard equality with God as something to be exploited, but emptied himself, taking the form of a slave, being born in human likeness' (Phil. 2.5-7). Traditionally, interpreters have highlighted the humility of the Son of God in becoming a human being. That's certainly the thrust of Paul's message. At the same time, the passage implies that Christ, who shared by right in all the glory and wonder of God the Father, became an ordinary human being. We see here that Christ is the opposite of those who seek to rob God by exchanging their ordinary lives with something more godlike. If Satan conned Adam and Eve with the temptation to become gods, then Christ saved us by choosing to become ordinary.

And, surely, one of the messages of the Gospel is this very ordinariness. Christ came into our world as an ordinary baby, born as babies always are, and to parents who, if not the peasants of medieval retellings, were still ordinary folk. He then spent almost all of his earthly life working as a typical craftsman. I've long been struck by the absurdity of the all-powerful and all-loving Son working for twenty years or more as a humble craftsman, probably of no reputation or help to anyone beyond Nazareth and its surroundings. As Johnny Cash sang in 1969 at Madison Square Garden, Jesus was a carpenter like any other, 'But he put aside his tools and He walked the burning highways / To build a house from folks like me and you.'[4] Jesus the commonplace carpenter builds a house (not a castle or mansion) from ordinary folks. The historical appeal of our ordinary Saviour to ordinary people can't be exaggerated.

That ordinariness didn't end, though, with the start of his Messianic ministry at his baptism. He may have spoken with authority and performed wonders, but he did so among the ordinary folk of Palestine. His contacts with the high and mighty were rare and almost never of his own choosing. Christ is striking in his almost complete indifference to status, as though he could see the *person* so clearly that he was blind to earthly trappings. His teachings and parables were most often about common things – sheep, wine, water, bread, fish and wheat – and even his death was that of a common criminal in an uninteresting corner of the Roman Empire. There's also an ordinariness to his Resurrection: he rose from the tomb in the springtime of a garden when we expect dead things to blossom into new life.

Similarly, while Christians have always been drawn to and fascinated by the great saints and figures of the church, the reality is that the Kingdom of God has been built in the monotony of human life. The people we should honour are less the great saints – who by and large are probably embarrassed by our veneration – than the ordinary faithful who simply persevered in remaining faithful to their God day in and day out during the daily experiences of their unremarkable lives. Give me the parents worn out from sleepless nights by a colicky child who nevertheless attend church each Sunday; or the woman who puts up with an ungrateful husband and yet praises God in her daily prayers; the elderly couple who overcome their ailments to provide coffee after Sunday services or to visit people in hospitals. In lives such as these, we encounter

---

[4]Johnny Cash, 'Jesus was a carpenter', https://www.lyrics.com/lyric/19556431/Jesus+Was+a+Carpenter, accessed 18 July 2020.

extraordinary faith and devotion in the ordinary – we might say real – lives of men and women. That's where God's wonder and glory are most visible. He manifests himself in a thousand ways we fail to appreciate because, well, it's just too ordinary for us.

What this and Christ's own ministry teach us is that living properly within the commonplace experience of life requires humility. 'Let the same mind be in you that was in Christ Jesus' compels us to swim against the current of human grasping after fame and glory. We tend to think of humility as self-abnegation, the playing down of our own talents and virtues or perhaps proverbially tugging our forelocks to our betters. Humility thus becomes something hard to square with modern ideas of self-esteem – there's a fine line between virtuous humility and a debilitating lack of confidence. As we see in Philippians 2, self-abnegation or (in theological terminology) self-emptying is very much a part of how we understand humility, but that same tradition also condemns false modesty as a form of deceit. Real humility begins with honesty.

Humility involves recognizing our limits and capacities, and then constraining ourselves accordingly. To do this, we must take a proper account of ourselves, marking not only our strengths and weaknesses but also the many ways we're inclined to take more than we ought and to exaggerate our own importance over others. Jealousy, defensiveness, criticism and acquisitiveness are fruits of pride, and they reveal that a lack of humility can lead not only to arrogance but also to a diminished sense of self-worth. Essentially, humility involves accepting gladly that we are finite, fallible creatures. It allows us to celebrate our own creatureliness and to cease comparing ourselves to others. It has also traditionally been associated with temperance, or the virtue of living within our means. Both humility and temperance direct us to embrace the ordinary in our lives by recognizing our limits as creatures and our need to live charitably with our neighbours. By seeking to live modestly, we restrain our desire to stand out from and rise above our neighbours – we recognize that our deepest needs are met not in competition with them (or God) but by loving our neighbours as ourselves.

According to Thomas Aquinas, to be humble we 'must know [our] disproportion to that which surpasses [our] capacity'.[5] Anyone who

---

[5]Thomas Aquinas, *The Summa Theologica of St. Thomas Aquinas*, Vol. 2 (New York: Benzinger Brothers, 1947), II-II.qu.161.a.2.

has thru-hiked knows what Aquinas means. One of my favourite parts of trekking is my preparation beforehand. I pore over maps, make an inventory of all that's needed for the journey, weigh each item considering its worth versus its weight and assess what I'm really capable of accomplishing in altitude and distance each day. When you're carrying everything on your back, you have to think clearly about your planning. It's no good exaggerating the weight you can bear or the distance over broken ground you can cover. Reality on the trail will cruelly dash any delusions of grandeur you might have with painful blisters, sore muscles, exhaustion or worse. Exchanging glory for safety is a prerequisite for mountaineering – only those who can turn back a few hundred feet from the summit should make the attempt. Humility is essentially doing the same with life.

The theologian Norman Wirzba has a concept that aligns closely with Aquinas's definition of humility: the 'art of the commonplace'. In his introduction to *The Art of the Commonplace: the Agrarian Essays of Wendell Berry*, he locates the 'commonplace' at the heart of our recovery of a more sustainable and harmonious way of living:

> Clearly what is needed is the recovery of the sense that our lives are necessarily and beneficially tied to the well-being of the earth, that the earth and its inhabitants form one vast 'commonplace'. In this recovery, two basic transformations must occur. On the one hand, we must learn to think differently about the aims of life, of what counts as valuable knowledge or a noble pursuit. . . . On the other hand, we must learn to reorganize our economic and social lives around the principle that health is an all-inclusive concept, a concept that involves soil, water, plants, animals, ecosystems, individuals, families, cities, and nations.[6]

Later, he adds that a prerequisite for recovering the 'art of the commonplace' is the 'taming of our desire to the scale of the earth'.[7] In other words, learning to delight in the ordinary, finding satisfaction in our participation in the common creaturehood of all living things, requires humility. Our ordinary lives aren't second

---

[6]Norman Wirzba, *The Art of the Commonplace: The Agrarian Essays of Wendell Berry* (Berkeley: Counterpoint, 2002), xv–xvi.
[7]Ibid., xvi.

best, the sorry lot of those who've never achieved fame, wealth or adoration. In fact, compared to the majority of people who have lived or are alive today, we in the West have already achieved most of those things. Rather, we need the wisdom to see that it's precisely in the commonplace that we can discover true happiness and lasting satisfaction. Only the sirens of our own age pretend otherwise, and even then, only so that they may profit from our own discontentment.

-o0o-

One person who definitely would not have approved of my nomadic lifestyle was St Benedict. In his *Rule*, he heaped scorn on *gyrovagues*, 'who spend their entire lives drifting from region to region. . . . Always on the move, they never settle down, and are slaves to their own wills and gross appetites. . . . It is better to keep silent than to speak of all these and their disgraceful way of life.'[8] Unlike the monks of Ireland and Anglo-Saxon England who made *peregrinatio*, or wandering, central to their pursuit of holiness, Benedict stressed *stabilitas* or staying put in a self-sufficient community for all of one's life. Alongside fidelity and obedience, stability is one of the vows that Benedictine monks are required to make before entering a monastery. In a world crashing down around him following the fall of Rome, Benedict understandably believed that perfection and holiness are best pursued in the company of a stable, local community.

In her superb little book on Benedictine spirituality, Esther de Waal explains why stability is essential:

> The Benedictine recognition of the role of stability is not a piece of idealism, it is essentially realistic. Everyone needs to feel at home, to feel earthed, for it is impossible to say, 'Who am I?' without first asking, 'Where am I? When have I come? Where am I going?' Without roots we can neither discover where we belong nor can we grow. Without stability we cannot confront the basic questions of life. Without stability we cannot know

---

[8]Benedict of Nursia, *The Rule of St. Benedict in English*, ed. O. S. B. Timothy Fry (Collegeville: The Liturgical Press, 1982), 1.10-12.

our true selves. For we are pulled apart by so many conflicting demands, so many things deserving our attention, that often it seems as though the centre cannot hold.[9]

To embrace the commonplace is to honour the places where we live but not at the expense of all the other places where others live. Stability is the virtue necessary for inhabiting the paradoxes we've explored – eternity and history, silence and words – in the particular places we live and to find in them something that's both utterly unique but also common to creation. De Waal continues:

> Instead of the bewildering and exhausting rushing from one thing to another monastic stability means accepting this particular community, this place and these people, this and no other, as the way to God. The man or woman who voluntarily limits himself or herself to one building and a few acres of ground for the rest of life is saying that contentment and fulfilment do not consist in constant change, that true happiness cannot necessarily be found anywhere other than in this place and this time.[10]

Settling down, resting from the constant busyness of modern life, practising living well with our God, our places and our neighbours, learning the art of the commonplace – what, in the end, could be more wonderful than that?

---

[9]Esther de Waal, *Seeking God: The Way of St. Benedict* (Collegeville: The Liturgical Press, 1984), 56–7.
[10]Ibid., 57.

10

The Eucharist

I bade farewell to Cadair Idris. As of my writing this chapter, I've been back only once – a brief visit when heavy rain and an impenetrable fog convinced my wife and me to venture no further than the car park. What surprises me most isn't that I've not climbed up to the craggy Penygadair in over five years (Wales has plenty of mountains and countryside to explore elsewhere), but that Cadair Idris has continued to tickle my imagination for so long. Since that overnight trip, I've been up many more mountains, a number of which are far more impressive in size and sublimity. Cadair Idris hardly compares to the cols of the Tour du Mont Blanc or the otherworldly peaks in Iceland where glacial heights loom over lunar landscapes. And yet Cadair Idris has occupied a place in my memories like no other mountain.

Perhaps it was some premonition of this impact that made me particularly reflective as I drove back to Cardiff in South Wales. A much more likely cause was the juxtaposition between what I'd discovered on the slopes and heights of Cadair Idris and my ordinary life back home. For about twenty-four hours, I'd escaped the stress of my job, the emotions that were seeping from my failed marriage, and anxieties about my impending move to Oxford. Something about my immersion in that wilderness had grounded me, but it had undoubtedly also allowed me to park the psychological burden I'd long been carrying, as though exchanging it briefly for the weight of my rucksack. Now that I'd taken the pack off and dropped it heavily into the back of my car, I could feel that emotional burden returning. It wouldn't be so easily shifted now.

Oddly enough, however, as I pulled onto the main road and left the Dysynni Valley behind me, it wasn't the contrast between my ordinary life and the joy of the last two days that preoccupied me. Out of nowhere came quite a different thought. I was listening to a programme on the car radio about technology, the razzle-dazzle of some new game or show (I can't now remember the details) that everyone was raving about. Some wag compared it to seeing Star Wars for the first time and judged for the viewers that it was unlike anything that they will have experienced in their real lives. I thought of the U2 song 'Better than the real thing' and suddenly had an epiphany that has since completely changed how I think of wonders.

Since at least the early twentieth century, we've tried to outdo nature and the past with our wonders. Beavers build dams. Well, take a look at our Hoover Dam. Sure, the Romans built some amazing buildings, but just take a look at the Empire State Building. You can see this mentality clearly displayed in promotion postcards printed to celebrate the building of the Titanic that revel in its size compared with famous monuments or a sailing ship. Man-made marvels are often the result of ingenuity (like a technological invention), or exaggeration (like a skyscraper), or special effect (like a light show). They double as monuments to man, which is why modernity has been besotted with creating wonders, scaling them upwards as their designers try to outdo their rivals and predecessors. Apart from art and craftsmanship (I'll get to that soon), our manufactured wonders usually impose themselves forcefully on the natural world. They strive to achieve what nature can't or stand at odds with ordinary notions of beauty and form (as I heard an architect once describe it). They're fashioned to gain our attention, impress us and garner praise for those who design and build them. Each is, if you will, a new effort at building Babel.

This impulse to experience unearthly wonders has, if anything, become even more pervasive since the dawn of advanced computing. The games we play, the blockbuster movies we watch, the online worlds we explore and even the doctored images of people we view deliberately seek to outdo anything we might encounter in the real world. For our pleasure, we want to consume spectacles – even if only in a virtual way – that are as far removed as possible from our ordinary lives and places. Why settle for the nearby countryside when you can cinematically explore a stunning fantasy world? Why settle for the earth when there are 'new worlds and new civilizations' designed to dazzle us? Why deal with messy relationships with people burdened with blemished faces when you can be gratified by extraordinary men and women online? So much of our entertainment industry hooks audiences by offering fantastical wonders that nature could never in a million years produce.

Years ago, when I was providing a young man with spiritual direction, I was struck by this power of the virtual to draw people away from the natural. After hearing me one Sunday morning explain contemplative prayer, he wanted to give it a try. But it quickly became clear that he found even a few minutes of silence extremely burdensome. Though he never expressed it in these terms, the problem was that he found it boring. As we talked about the issue, it suddenly occurred to me that his lifestyle was the real problem. He lived within a stone's throw of Pisgah National Forest, some of the most beautiful countryside and wilderness you could hope to explore, and yet he hardly ever stepped foot in it. Instead, he spent almost all of his leisure time playing video games or watching TV. How extraordinary, I thought, that he should sit indoors exploring imaginary worlds mediated through pixels rather than the real and glorious one outside. When I asked him about that, his reply was, 'The games are more fun.' He was nearly thirty years old.

It would be easy to laugh at this, shake our heads and grumble about youth today. But really, he was living only as he had been trained. A steady diet of ever-changing wonders – from the magic of plentiful food available with only a swipe of a card to the cornucopia of computer games – inured him even to the spectacular beauty of the Appalachian Mountains. From almost any perspective but our own, his life was suffused with wonders. Every aspect of his middle-class lifestyle was supplied by a global industry engineered to provide him a reliably steady diet of marvels that kings and queens of old would have envied. The result of this – as with almost all of us in one way or another – was to make the extraordinary ordinary and everything else boring.

Most of these man-made wonders require little if any adaptation on our part because they've been specifically engineered to attract us. We don't accidentally find them wonderful – they've been designed and promoted with us in mind. When I encouraged this young man to force himself to go for walks in the countryside, to visit Looking Glass Falls or go swimming in the cool waters of the Davidson River, he could never quite manage to get around to it. His life had become so saturated with pleasures designed to attract and engage him that he was like an addict trying through self-discipline to give up drugs. The magic of technology, ingenuity and marketing hooked him into a world of unreality, one which incidentally requires an enormous outlay of resources to provide.

How different from this are natural wonders. When I stood admiring my 360° panorama atop Cadair Idris, what dominated my view could be summed up by the old terrestrial elements: earth, water, air, fire. The igneous rocks that had caught my attention during my ascent comprise 90–95 per cent of the earth's crust. They're 'as common as muck' as they might say in northern England. The peaty turf here still seems exotic to me but effectively it's grass, which we can see almost anywhere. The rest was primarily liquid water, vapour, air and the sun. I could go on, but you get the picture. Natural wonders always consist of the most ordinary, most common of materials, only arranged and displayed in ways that catch our attention and amaze us. Effectively, they're reminders that we don't wonder enough – that Mother Nature is forced to go to extremes to get us to experience the wonder that came easily to us when we were small children.

The ordinariness of natural wonders teaches us at least two lessons. The first should now be a familiar theme: natural wonders exist harmoniously with the rest of creation. My admiration of mossy stones alongside a babbling brook or the scent of honeysuckle on an early summer's day costs the planet nothing. Natural marvels are nothing other than ordinary things that strike us human beings in particular ways. There was nothing objectively different within my mountaintop view from many other places. Nothing had been imposed there; nothing was *alien* to the landscape. The sea had simply filled the gap left by Ireland and Britain sliding apart, the river flowed from a spring somewhere up the mountains, the rock and earth were formed by typical geological forces and the vegetation had sprouted (as it always does) from rich, fertile soil. Nothing was done with any intention, except perhaps by God. The landscape was simply formed over aeons in the same general way that every other untouched inch of our world has reached its present state.

What was different was the natural arrangement of air, water, earth and fire in a way that clothed everything with beauty. My vantage from almost 3,000 feet allowed me to see that arrangement as a whole, like stepping back to appreciate the entirety of a painting or an architectural masterpiece. Perhaps a better way of thinking about this is to say that my vista allowed me to see in a different dimension. Nothing had been imposed or rearranged with the intention of gaining my attention. But the dimension of beauty enabled me to see the wonder of ordinary things – form imbued even dull rock and earth with majesty.

But, as they say, beauty is in the eye of the beholder; my view was available only to those with discerning eyes (and strong legs): that is, people who stand atop Cadair Idris and take in the view. Natural wonders really exist only in the human mind. In and of themselves, they're completely ordinary and unusual. If scientists were to catalogue everything within my mountaintop view and list their primary properties, not one single thing would be remarkable. Water remains H_2O in whatever state it comes – but how different to us is a thundering waterfall from the trickle of a faucet. Yet, how ordinary is the water itself.

The second lesson takes us back to G. K. Chesterton's idea that we're too old to marvel at everyday things – our sense of wonder is too thin to discover the wonderful in anything but the spectacular. Our world is filled with wonders that we're too bored to notice. We often don't appreciate things that would dazzle people who'd never come across them before, like Floridians thrilled by the appearance of a few snowflakes. The familiar isn't wonderful unless something extraordinary makes it so. We're too preoccupied or too demanding to delight in the everyday. We need something spectacular to jolt us out of our imaginative malaise. Otherwise, we take familiar marvels for granted. I'm reminded of this whenever I return from trekking. How delightful a comfortable bed, a home-cooked meal, a cushioned sofa and a proper toilet become when you've gone without them. How astonishing is the warmth of the sun when you live in mid-Wales.

Few people have better articulated our typical failure to appreciate the commonplace than the seventeenth-century poet Thomas Traherne. The dual themes of his *Centuries of Meditations* are the astonishing wonder to be found in ordinary things and how delighting in them is the key to a rich and contented life. He captures these ideas in a phrase he repeats like a litany: 'You never enjoy the world aright till . . .' For example,

You never enjoy the world aright, till you see how a sand exhibiteth the wisdom and power of God: And prize in everything the service which they do you, by manifesting His glory and goodness to your Soul; far more than the visible beauty on their surface, or the material services they can do for your body . . . to take pleasure in all the benefits it doth to all is Heavenly, for so they do in Heaven. To do so is to be divine and good, and to imitate our Infinite and Eternal Father.[1]

Elsewhere, he writes, 'Your enjoyment of the world is never right, till every morning you awake in Heaven; see yourself in your Father's Palace: and look upon the skies, the earth, and the air as Celestial Joys: having such a reverend esteem of all, as if you were among the Angels.'[2] And finally, 'You never enjoy the world aright, till the Sea itself floweth in your veins, till you are clothed with the heavens, and crowned with the stars: and perceive yourself to be the sole heir of the whole world, and more so, because men are in it who are every one sole heirs as well as you.'[3] Traherne pushes us to recognize that there really is no 'ordinary', that all of creation can be a source of joy if we would only stop to appreciate it. To paraphrase Augustine, miracles seem so only to those who forget that existence itself is miraculous.

Traherne was trying to help us see that wonder and the commonplace appear as opposites only within a jaundiced perspective, that our capacity to delight in the everyday may have atrophied. Some might say that this is inevitable, that it's part of our human nature to prefer some things to others, to be moved by places and experiences that seem special to us because they're rare and beautiful. Everything else is either too ordinary for us to appreciate as marvels (though we may still occasionally cherish their beauty if we're in the right mood) or not sufficiently unusual to stand out and make us notice them. Part of this is due to context – the rain I moan about in Wales would amaze anyone living in a desert climate – but much of it has to do, as Traherne recognized, with our perspective and expectations. We effectively have to be trained to delight in the commonplace.

---

[1]Traherne, *Centuries*, 1:27.
[2]Ibid., 1:28.
[3]Ibid., 1:29.

The artist Paul Cézanne recognized this final point and dedicated his life to learning how to appreciate nature for itself and to delight in his perception of it. He had an almost religious fervour in his approach to trying to capture the beauty of everyday objects. 'I will astonish Paris with an apple,' he once declared.[4] As his painting matured, he stopped mimicking the techniques of earlier masters and turned, instead, to nature itself for his teacher. He explained:

> Imagination is a very beautiful thing; but it must have a firm base. As for myself, when I came into contact with the Impressionists, I realized that I had to become a student of the world again, to make myself a student once more. I no more imitated Pizarro and Monet than I did the masters in the Louvre. I tried to produce work which was my own, work which was sincere, naïve, in accordance with my abilities and my vision.[5]

He painted the same still-life objects repeatedly as he strove to convey on canvas something of the sensations that impressed themselves on his senses. Often, the fruits and flowers in the bowl had decayed before he was satisfied. This painter, who faithfully attended Mass but disliked priests, pronounced nature to be God's 'catechism', by which he meant, I suppose, that nature teaches us how to appreciate itself and see God.

Cézanne struggled to experience nature as an artist in a direct way, to admire it for itself rather than for how it had been depicted by other artists. Proper art, he wrote, is 'nature expressed through a temperament . . . which is disciplined, which can organize its sensations'.[6] Artists, in his view, are those who devote themselves to directing their whole being towards conveying nature's own authenticity. As Norman Wirzba notes, the artist is a communicator of nature, seeking through his or her own perceptions to bear witness to the 'life and movement and mystery' of the world around

---

[4]Quoted in Michael Doran, ed., *Conversations with Paul Cézanne* (Berkley: UC Press, 2001), xx.
[5]Richard Kendall, *Cézanne by Himself* (London: Time Warner Books, 2004), 196.
[6]Ibid.

us.[7] There's a touch of the priestly vocation in Cézanne's artist: only by devoting himself totally to perceiving the ordinary world can he manifest that world to those otherwise blind.

But he didn't naively think this was an easy task. The artist's senses have to be 'organized', disciplined, to focus on what they're perceiving. Such disciplining requires dedication and a kind of introspective wisdom. Artists, he believed, are particularly prone to prostitute themselves for the sake of praise and fame. Perhaps because critics had so often been brutal in their assessment of his work, Cézanne could be harshly critical of more successful artists. But he also seems to have harboured a deep disdain for artistic hypocrisy:

> In order to make progress, there is only nature, and the eye is trained through contact with her. . . . One can do good things without being very much of a harmonist or a colourist. It is sufficient to have a sense of art. . . . Therefore institutions, pensions, honours can only be made for cretins, humbugs and rascals. Don't be an art critic, but paint, there lies salvation.[8]

Honest communication requires discipline and training through long exposure to the depth and mystery of nature. Cézanne practised what he preached, spending countless hours focused on the objects he was studying. He drew and painted them from different angles, in different lights and at varying distances. He was, as it were, exposing himself as fully as possible to the unfathomable mystery contained in any one view, be it Mount Sainte Victoire, a still life of a bowl of fruit or a riverbank.

We can learn from Cézanne something about what might be called the adventure of the commonplace. What do I mean by this? Let's begin with wonders. There's something awfully easy about them. Almost anyone can be deeply moved by a grand view from a mountaintop or by golden rays of a sunset licking the waves of a darkening ocean. It would take a heart of cold stone not to be deeply moved by such scenes. You might say these are examples of creation revealing itself in ways that even amateurs can appreciate. No work of the imagination

---

[7] Ibid., 61.
[8] Ibid., 159.

or disciplining of the senses is necessary. Even those impervious to natural beauty can't long resist the truly spectacular, like when I took my teenage son to the Alps for the first time.

Perceiving wonder in the commonplace, however, requires intentionality. We must be determined to perceive it, forcing our wandering attention to be still long enough to discern the beauty and wonder that lie in ordinary things. And this takes discipline too – we can only learn to appreciate ordinary things by training our senses to be continually mindful of their inherent worth. It was only when I stepped away from the computer screen and television that I began to discover all the commonplace gems of my life – from the food I cooked for my family each day, the joy of sharing the company of friends and family, to the beauty I could enjoy in my backyard. I had known all these things before but had taken them for granted and rarely stopped to appreciate them properly and regularly. I had to stop and notice before I could begin to enjoy the world aright.

Cézanne demonstrates how art can be a means for disciplining our perceptions to find the wonder of the commonplace. The artistic eye, at its best, is one that has been trained through long, hard work to see everyday beauty. The desire to communicate such beauty to others is what motivates many people to develop their artistic talents and create their own marvels that draw our attention to what we would otherwise overlook. Ever since I began admiring Cézanne's still-lifes, my eyes have been opened to the actual still-lifes I encounter in my everyday life: I regularly stop to admire the arrangement of fruit and vegetables in our earthenware bowl in our kitchen. His paintings have encouraged me to delight in something as simple as apples, bananas, a few onions and a head of garlic gathered in a bowl. I dare you to place a price on that simple pleasure.

Similarly, husbandry and craftsmanship teach us to engage with the commonplace in ways that attune our senses to its wonder. The work of the husbandman or the craftsman requires a capacity for delight in mundane tasks since almost all such work necessarily involves routine and tedium – that is to say, it involves hard work. Masons must chip away at their stone patiently, weavers work their techniques repetitively, potters spin their wheels and shape clay over and over again and musicians rehearse the same piece of music until listeners want to cry. I quietly admire my wife's patience when she knits. It looks mind-bogglingly tedious to me and yet how lovely are its fruits.

Good gardeners work with nature, adding nothing that doesn't nurture soil, roots, fruit and flower, to arrange ordinary plants into something wonderful. Farmers who haven't been forced to use industrial methods learn to know their land, animals and crops well enough to encourage their flourishing. Wendell Berry writes:

> Correct discipline cannot be hurried, for it is both the knowledge of what ought to be done, and the willingness to do it – *all* of it, properly. The good worker will not suppose that good work can be made properly answerable to haste, urgency, or even emergency. But the good worker knows too that after it is done work requires yet more time to prove its worth. One must stay to experience and study and understand the consequences – must understand them by living with them, and then correct them, if necessary, by longer living and more work.[9]

In all these examples (and many more), people demonstrate an earthy wisdom fertilized by patience and humility that recognizes that our truest wonders don't strive to eclipse nature but, rather, help her ordinary elements stand out in sharper splendour or fruitfulness. They all work patiently alongside nature to produce wonders from commonplace objects. And those committed to such work derive from the earth a deep satisfaction that costs our planet little or nothing. What greater source of happiness can there be than this?

Such artists, gardeners, craftsmen and farmers teach us, like Traherne's meditations, that perceiving wonder in the commonplace is essential for our social well-being. Only by appreciating and adjusting ourselves to ordinary things can we ever begin to solve the most pressing issues of our day. All our solutions to climate change and ecological destruction will only be temporary if we remain addicted to spectacles and striving for extraordinary lives. Our planet can't cope with billions of people expecting it to provide easy marvels or delights without drudgery. As long as we believe it's our right to escape ordinary lives, we won't begin to truly cherish

---

[9]Wendell Berry, 'People, Land, and Community', in Norman Wirzba, *The Art of the Commonplace*, 187.

and live properly on an extraordinary planet. Our world wasn't made to meet such high expectations and insatiable demands.

Currently, however, we revel in a society that increasingly requires more than God thought sufficient to give us; we live in what Postmodern philosophers call the age of the spectacle. Having deadened our hearts to the delight of God exhibited in everyday lives and things, we yearn for an unrealistic world that keeps us continually supplied with hits of the spectacular. Mundane wonders lie all around us; commonplace things that are marvels in their own right constantly fail to catch our attention. So, we continue our search for the spectacular like children at the fairground drifting from one attraction to the next. We've been trained to never be satisfied with anything for long. Spectacles soon become familiar, and then we move on in our psychologically nomadic life in search of new and better wonders to consume. By such means have we become the world's locusts rather than her stewards.

-o0o-

And so, at last we come to our final juxtaposition: atop Cadair Idris I could see nothing that wasn't commonplace: sky, sun, earth, rock, water, air, grass. There wasn't a single object in my view that I wouldn't find in my own garden back home. And yet how wonderful it all was. In the ordinariness of this world, I encountered God's glory; in the wonder of that glory, I could see only what's available anywhere. The wonderful and the mundane, together, inseparable and utterly overwhelming my defences.

With a little theological imagination, you might say that my view was a topographical parable about the Incarnation: the wonderful and the ordinary are united in Jesus in a way that overcomes our defences. The incomprehensible majesty of God and the utter ordinariness of a human being, the divine and creaturely, united in Christ. But what I also learned as I reflected on the commonplace wonder of Cadair Idris is how unremarkable the Incarnation really is; it reminds us that creation always stands ready to receive her Lord. Much has been made over the centuries of how strange it was that God should become a human being. But perhaps the Babe of Bethlehem only seems extraordinary to us too blinded by sin to recognize that God never stands at a distance from his creation and that creation has always yearned to embrace her Creator. If 'creation waits with eager longing for the revealing of the children of God' (Rom. 8.19), then how much more does she yearn for her Lord? Perhaps the Fall did not so much estrange the world from God as us from both God and the community of creation.

At the start of Book Five of his *Confessions*, Augustine reflected on how during his dissolute youth he was blind to God even though God was everywhere around him. Even as he searched for God, God was actually near to him (closer, as he notes later, than he was even to himself). He concludes: 'Where was I when I was seeking for you? You were there before me, but I had departed from myself. I could not even find myself, much less you.'[10] Here, Augustine echoes and develops Paul at the start of Romans:

> Ever since the creation of the world his eternal power and divine nature, invisible though they are, have been understood and seen through the things he has made. So they are without excuse; for though they knew God, they did not honor him as God or give thanks to him, but they became futile in their thinking, and their senseless minds were darkened. Claiming to be wise, they became fools. (Rom. 1.20-22)

Augustine perceived what we so often fail to see: not only that we have absented ourselves from the God who is all around and in us but also that by so doing we became lost to ourselves. The Incarnation declares, as in our marriage services, that those whom God has joined together, let no one separate. God and his creation are never apart; it's only us fallen human beings, in our pride and self-centredness, who came to believe otherwise.

The dark truth of modernity is that once we lose sight of God, we soon lose sight of the creation and of ourselves. We become lost souls in a darkening world no longer hallowed by the presence of God. Our desperate search for wonders and pleasurable escapes from the familiar is more like addicts turning their place inside out to find drugs than a search for something divine. In our bid to create wonderful lives on our own terms, we've lost touch with our Creator and are swiftly destroying his creation. The Incarnation demonstrated, however, that despite our perceived isolation, the

---

[10]Augustine, *Confessions*, 5.2.2.

wonder of God is commonplace and that all that is ordinary is taken up in the majesty of God. I'm not suggesting that God becoming man wasn't unique, but it wasn't a violation, an invasion, a rupture in the divine order of creation – the Incarnation was creation's summation, calling us like prodigal children back into the fold.

But, if I may press a little further, I think the relationship between the wonderful and the commonplace is fundamentally Eucharistic. The old prayer of Thomas Aquinas, said in many churches before the Eucharist, begins with: 'O God, who in a wonderful sacrament . . .' Certainly, it is a 'wonderful sacrament', but it's an utterly ordinary thing, too. In the unremarkable substance of bread and wine we encounter and receive the wonder of Christ's presence. In the everyday practice of people gathering for a meal we find the world's Saviour in our midst. What's more common than grapes, water and wheat, what food more commonplace than bread, what place more unexceptionable than a table set for a meal? And yet in that place and in these items, the faithful discover their wonderful Saviour and are united with God. No flashy eloquence of a preacher here; no spectacle of a multimedia show; no wind, earthquake or fire – just the still, small voice of God in broken bread and wine outpoured.

If we accept that we've become estranged from both God and his creation, then we can also see how fitting it is that we're united with God through ordinary elements. If God had come dressed only in his majesty, then we'd be forgiven for embracing wonders with no thought for the everyday. In essence, he would be confirming the human compulsion to grasp after power and glory. Conversely, if the bread and wine were only barren signs of Christ, nothing more than mementos of his body and blood, then we could continue to consider wonders and the commonplace – heaven and earth – as regions distant from each other. But the Eucharist declares to us that what God has joined together can never be separated, that in Christ even ordinary people are welcome to be transformed into extraordinary creatures.

In his beautiful little book *For the Life of the World*, the Orthodox theologian Alexander Schmemann writes:

In this world Christ is crucified, His Body broken, and His Blood shed. And we must go out of this world, we must ascend to heaven in Christ in order to become partakers of the world to come. But this is not an 'other' world, different from the one God has created and given to us. It is our same world, *already* perfected in Christ, but *not yet* in us. It is our same world, redeemed and restored, in which Christ 'fills all things with Himself'. And since God has created the world as food for us and has given us food as a means of communion with Him, of life in Him, the new food of the new life which we receive from God in His Kingdom *is Christ himself*. He is our bread – because from the very beginning all our hunger was a hunger for Him and all our bread but a symbol of Him, a symbol that had to become a reality.[11]

My mountaintop experience on Cadair Idris demonstrated the truth of this. The wonder I witnessed there wasn't an escape from the ordinary but a movement deeper into it. Likewise, the Incarnation reveals that our salvation doesn't involve a flight from this world but rather an ascent to God *through* the world he created, redeemed and transformed. So too, the Eucharist invites us to the marriage feast of the Lamb by receiving Christ's extraordinary presence in ordinary food. As with contemplation, the path to God lies in our moving upwards by moving inwards – not just into our own souls but into the reality of God graciously wedded to his creation.

If baptism resolves the paradox of silence and words, then the Eucharist should engender in us an appreciation for the ordinariness of God's presence and the wonder to be found in the most commonplace of things. The Eucharist ought also to tell us something crucial about our humanity: we are ordinary creatures each wonderfully made. It's beyond time for us to live like that's true, not by grasping after things that may make our lives extraordinary nor in a desperate competition with the natural world, our neighbours and God. Look around at the fruits of that approach: a world and society teetering on the edge of ecological collapse. No, it's time for us to enjoy Christ's banquet set amid his creation and to discover there the abounding love of our wonderful Saviour proudly arrayed in ordinary humanity, who gladly comes to us in bread and wine. As the poet George Herbert reminds us in his famous poem 'Love (III)', Love bids us welcome to that feast; Love also heals and restores us so we may eat at the feast; we have only to sit and eat.

---

[11] Alexander Schmemann, *For the Life of the World* (Crestwood: St Vladimir's Press, 1998), 42–3.

11

Inhabiting *Hiraeth* and *Tangnefedd*

To an extent, my overnight trek on Cadair Idris was unremarkable. I've enjoyed far more awe-inspiring walks in other wildernesses that have required more from me physically and mentally or have filled me with greater wonder. I wouldn't even say that it was my favourite overnight trek in Snowdonia – that accolade goes to a night spent atop Pen yr Ole Wen in northwest Wales where I sat alone watching the sunset beyond the Isle of Anglesey, gradually giving way to a starry sky. But few walks have left as deep an impression as that autumnal ascent up Cadair Idris. Why?

That has been my own exploration in writing this book: to answer why those few miles on Cadair Idris stand out so powerfully from the other 20,000 miles I've hiked over the years. The reason can't be found in its scenery. That's beautiful for sure, but it's no different from the rest of Snowdonia and, frankly, doesn't compare to Norwegian fjords, the Alps, the high Pyrenees or other places I've trekked. The sense of history was certainly remarkable and undoubtedly touches on the reason why I was so affected, but can't itself be the cause. Here in my home in Brecon, I'm surrounded by a heritage just as rich and evocative. Neither was the trek especially taxing; I didn't complete my route with the satisfaction of having overcome physical challenges that forced me to 'dig deep' into myself, to use that well-worn cliché of endurance athletes.

Take all these things, though, and add them to the season of my life during that autumn of 2015, and I think an answer to my question begins to take shape. I'm by nature a reflective person – perhaps too much so at times – as happy to dwell in my own head as among others. The more that stress and the pressures of life mount, the more thoughtful I become, though usually not in a depressive or morose way nor necessarily even in one that results in bouts of obsessive *self*-reflection. My thoughts don't typically become fixated on me and my own plight. Rather, I become consumed by a curiosity about the *solidities* of life and this world. I succumb to an almost Platonic impulse to get behind the surface of reality to consider its deeper and more enduring qualities and connections. These ruminations come out strongly in my walks, leaving me suspended in a reverie as I ponder ideas and meanings. Rightly or wrongly, I've always had a powerful sense of a more profound and enduring world that lies around us but that we're too blind, too distracted, to see.

I'm sensible enough, I think, to realize that often this world or these supposed deeper meanings exist only in my own head and that just as often these reflective searches are simply weird ways of distracting myself from worldly woes. Some turn to drink or drugs, others to sex and relationships and still others to binge eating – I take a cerebral turn, which is at once less exhilarating and less expensive than many other distractions. But occasionally, these moments also allow me to perceive connections or perspectives I would otherwise miss, like the paradoxes I encountered in the ancient landscape of Cadair Idris. And they invariably leave me with a sense of being rooted in something mysterious, enwrapped in something that has rich layers of meaning, even goodness, that extend far beyond my comprehension. Cadair Idris, a monumental mountain within its own landscape, is perhaps a craggy metaphor for this sentiment.

At such times, my reflections turn my walks into a kind of pilgrimage. The long ruminations that accompany me on those walks become an extended prayer with the natural landscape serving as both the road and the destination – if you will, both the journey and the shrine. And if I'm right about the presence of God in nature and nature's capacity to reveal her Creator, then the objects and scenes I observe function as relics just as much as any saint's bones. Perhaps they're even more powerful since they remind me that holiness can be found beyond the sanctity of any given human being or object. Holiness can be found out *there* in the glimpses of Eden manifested in the world's beauty and teeming life.

The season of my life towards the end of 2015 certainly provided plenty of stormy weather for me to endure. The pressure of work had mounted and left me physically and mentally exhausted. I had spent the better part of a year fighting to save my college from closure. Combined with the everyday work of running residential training for ordinands, providing pastoral care and support, learning the ropes of being a principal and undertaking and a heavy teaching load, my work hours had mounted far beyond my ability to manage. By the autumn, I had, with my colleagues, won the battle to save the college, but I had also lost the battle to save the programme. Two years of work helping to transform the institution into a relatively happy residential community of serious learning and formation now began to be turned in new directions. My sense of injustice and frustration had increased to an intolerable level, and thus I would soon be leaving for Oxford.

During that same year, my long and often turbulent marriage ended. It didn't do so in a dramatic way. There was no sudden revelation of infidelity or even vicious rows that left us tearful and seething. My then wife no longer found the support she needed in me, and I was too worn down and distracted by work and nearly eighteen years of giving that support to respond as she wanted. And so, our marriage ended not with fireworks but with an affectionate hug and a simple goodbye. But this season of my life also felt like a new beginning, though not one of my own choosing. With so much up in the air, it was no wonder that I was unconsciously searching for solidities. I needed something to grasp onto – what better than the solidity of a mountain? And so, I arrived at Llanfihangel-y-pennant in a thoughtful mood that could only have made my mountain ascent a kind of pilgrimage.

As I reflected on my two days on Cadair Idris, I became increasingly aware that the mountain had given me a gift. It had taught me about my faith and, thus, also about myself. It's as though during that two-day walk, the scattered shards of my life had been swept up and pieced back together to form a life and faith newly understood. For the first time, my love of nature, my devotion to walking and my Anglican faith came together as a seamless whole that would sustain me in the difficult months ahead. I thought I was at an ending, but little did I know that I would face another two years of stress and unhappiness before a proper new beginning was given to me in the form of a new love and a return to the Wales I'd come to cherish. But that's a story for another day.

What did I learn about my faith during my overnight journey up Cadair Idris and back down again? Strip away everything else from our faith and I think we encounter at its heart the juxtapositions I'd discovered: timelessness, thick time, deep silence, enlivening words, breathtaking wonder and the utterly commonplace. In the midst of these contradictories lies a way, a truth and a life that I find mysteriously and richly *humane*. It's the *way* because delighting in the interplay of these paradoxes leads towards an abiding love of both God and his creation; it's *truth* because it reveals a reality that encompasses both the heavenly and the earthly; and it's *life* because it demonstrates that we live best by serving God, his creation and each other. And if exulting in these deep paradoxes is to embrace the way, the truth and the life, then it must really be a way of embracing Christ in whom those paradoxes are resolved.

Cadair Idris taught me that the paradoxes of timelessness and time, silence and words, wonder and the commonplace don't contend with each other so that the heart of our faith is troubled and disturbed. Rather, they dance joyfully around each other, underpinning, informing and subsisting in ways that can only seem paradoxical to us (like the relationship between God the Father, the Son and the Holy Spirit). Call this sacramental or incarnational, this dance reminds us that God and creation aren't opposed, that our spirit and body should enjoy a nuptial love and that the fact that God became man explains everything.

What *is* contradictory is how we human beings insist on conducting our lives. We're the ones who can't tolerate contradictions, who want everything to be understandable, for one thing to overshadow another, to be simple and easily handled. For us, contradictions must ever be at odds – the opposing dualities of our lives – resolvable only by one mastering the other. We clutter our lives and imaginations with warring dualisms locked in a perpetual battle for domination. We set men against women, the Right against the Left, reason against emotion, science against religion, the spiritual against the material, the mind against the body and so on almost ad infinitum. We even cast aside all sense of proportion by embracing the absurdity of setting our solitary selves and our often trivial desires and demands against the far wider world in which we find ourselves.

By so doing, we stand apart from the seamless whole of interwoven paradoxes such as those I'd encountered on Cadair Idris, trying to live happy lives that neglect or devalue them. Perhaps this is because our fallen hearts relish the heady exultation of battle. We don't really want to be at peace, not if it means accepting difference and learning not only to live with but actually to delight and find meaning in those who seem entirely opposed to us. Truth and meaning are for us only one-sided (even when we claim otherwise) and subject to easy, straightforward explanation. The idea that truth may lie in paradox, in holding together seemingly contradictory propositions, is hard to grasp or explain and thus is unacceptable. But perhaps Christ's command to love our enemies is a reminder that truth isn't so easily judged, the way so simply revealed or the life so readily comprehended on our own terms. Perhaps we *need* to love our enemies in order to find meanings that escape our control and egotism.

-o0o-

Am I becoming a little too poetically opaque? Then think of it this way: what Cadair Idris taught me is that marriage is a better metaphor than warfare for understanding differences. The irony of my mountain pilgrimage is that in the midst of my own marital breakdown, I discovered that the idea of marriage lies at the heart of my faith and resolves the mystery of paradoxes. I realized through my encounters with timelessness, time, silence, words, wonder and the ordinary that while we can and often do think of differences in terms of opposition, we can also see them as being intended, even created, for each other. In marriage, two become one not by one absorbing or overshadowing the other (though that may often happen) but by their being so united in love that each person's very distinctiveness becomes a means for ever-deepening union. In marriage, two different individuals become one and yet in their unity remain distinct from each other. What is that but a paradox?

What if differences were made for each other? What if differences are there to allow us to identify ourselves *with* others rather than *against* them? This, I believe, is the first lesson of Scripture. 'In the beginning God created the heavens and the earth.' So opens the first chapter of Genesis and also, of course, the Bible. In Chapter 1, we're presented with an account of not only creation but also polarities: heaven and earth, light and darkness, land and sea, sun and moon, plants and animals, man and woman. One way of interpreting this is as an implicit message of opposition, almost of dualism. That's perhaps the way we're disposed to read it in an age conditioned by our notions of the Right versus the Left, progressives versus conservatives.

But the message of Genesis 1 is actually one of unity. God creates the heavens and the earth and light and darkness and then 'God saw that it was good'. *It* not *they*. God fashions the land and the sea, and again we're told that 'God saw that *it* was good'. Even when God creates the multitude of animals, the object of his delight remains singular: 'And God saw that *it* was good.' God next forms man and woman in his own unifying image before gazing upon every atom of his creation and again delighting in it as a whole: 'God saw everything that he had made, and indeed *it* was very good.'

It's therefore fitting that after completing this new world with the Garden of Eden, God's first worry, the first time his delight is diminished, is when he says, 'It is not good that the man should be alone.' So far, everything God has done has been wonderful, teeming with life and fecundity. Suddenly, in Genesis 2 he sees something that isn't delightful: Adam is alone. Unless he too can share in conjugal love, the world won't be utterly delightful. And so, God fashions Eve; her formation caps the perfect world of unifying differences as Adam comes to recognize and embrace 'bone of my bones and flesh of my flesh'.

A central and often overlooked message of Genesis is that difference doesn't mean opposition. Genesis presents all creatures before the Fall as being intended for each other, united by God's delight, by the fact that he gazes on their union and sees that it is good. Genesis pushes us to see the difference as unifying, even nuptial. The image isn't of warfare but of marriage. We aren't presented with true polarities: not heavens versus the earth, sun versus moon, land versus sea or man versus woman – rather, each is joined together as if in marriage to make a whole. Profoundly, the verse about Adam and Eve being joined by God after the Fall is really the central teaching of the Bible: 'What God has joined together, let no one separate.'

What joins them together is not the dry respect or cold tolerance of our own rhetoric of diversity. Instead, it's delight: fundamentally, God's delight. All our so-called polarities and dualisms are united in his delight. To him they are *it* rather than *they*, and he delights in that wholeness: 'And God saw that it is good' is just another way of saying 'And God delighted in it'. Norman Wirzba captures this sense: 'Creation's goodness – its beauty and splendour, the very quality about it that makes God pause to behold it in moments of rapt attention and appreciation – is a reflection of God's perception of it.'[1] God's perception is his delight. That these juxtapositions are portrayed in a nuptial light also suggests that God enjoys paradoxes. What keeps creation from fragmenting and spinning out into chaos is the delight that God took and continues to take in his creation.

God even permits living creation to return that delight by fulfilling his commandment to be fruitful and multiply. The nuptial union of differences can thus also be generative, abounding in flourishing life. Before the Fall, Adam and Eve share in that delight through their own unselfish love for each other, their care for Eden, the Holy of Holies of creation, and by their obedience to the God who delights in them. Bearing the image God, Adam and Eve in their nuptial union stand at the pinnacle of the nuptial union of creation – the delight God takes in them overflows into the delight they take in each other and the delight they experience in paradise.

Notice, too, what this does to our understanding of the Incarnation. Far from being an anomaly, a strangely creative way God went about redeeming us, the Incarnation is the ultimate nuptial act. In Christ, humanity and God are married. In Christ, heaven and earth come back together without one absorbing the other. The whole debate about the Person of Christ (how he's both God and man) that consumed the church during its first five centuries can be seen as the theological determination to say of the Son in the face of heretics: 'What God has joined together, let no one separate.' And the Scriptural vision of the New Creation where heaven and earth meet (symbolized most powerfully by Revelation's vision of the New Jerusalem) declares that just as we began so too will we end in nuptial unity. Scripture is like a Shakespearean comedy: like *Twelfth Night* or *A Midsummer Night's Dream* or *Love's Labour's Lost*, it ends with the healing of division and a happy marriage. No wonder that so many of Jesus' parables involve a wedding feast.

'What God has joined together, let no one separate' invites us to embrace a sacramental vision of being human. In the face of a fallen world, it asks us to strive in Christ to hold together heaven and creation, spirit and matter, humanity and God and the active and the contemplative. In Galatians, Paul writes, 'There is no longer Jew or Greek, there is no longer slave or free, there is no longer male

---

[1] Norman Wirzba, *From Nature to Creation: A Christian Vision for Understanding and Loving Our World* (Grand Rapids: Baker, 2015), 74.

and female; for all of you are one in Christ Jesus.' Early Christians, in fact, remained all of these things after their conversion, but now their differences found unity in Christ. By questioning each and every one of those identities, Paul declares that what God has joined together, let no one separate. Taking the Incarnation as our guide, therefore, we can say that what seems mutually opposed, what seems antithetical, what seems paradoxical, is in reality a seamless whole, a deep unity redolent with divinity.

Reflecting on my overnight walk on Cadair Idris convinced me that this nuptial vision is central to Christianity. I've never looked at my Christian faith in the same way again. Suddenly, my love of history and the countryside, my enjoyment of stories and of contemplative silence and my delight in discovering mundane wonders all came together with my faith. I drove away from Cadair Idris, in the midst of a collapsing life, feeling more grounded and purposeful than ever. I knew that I would make it through it all because I had discovered in all those paradoxes not only a renewal of my faith but also my home.

-o0o-

The funny thing about my mountaintop epiphany is that it took so long to happen. I have spent most of my life reading history, most of my adulthood studying and writing theology and the greater part of the last fifteen years walking and hiking. I should have been aware of the paradoxes sooner than I was, even granted that I'm not always the swiftest person off the mark. But I was thinking like too many Christians today. I'd spent so long keeping God separate from his creation that I was blind to their close neighbourliness. God was the focus of my prayers, my research, my worship and my priestly vocation; the study of history was my pastime; walking my delight and my escape. But they didn't come together, until I *inhabited* that mountain landscape, if only for two days.

To inhabit, to live in a place, is to immerse yourself in its character and personality. Our relationship within a space or among a people is different from the relationship we have when we stand apart. When we stand apart from the things we observe, we take on an alien perspective, guarding ourselves from their influence, ensuring that we're in command. But when we inhabit a place, even for a short period, we find that distancing harder to achieve or maintain. There are too many forces at work on us to remain easily unaffected.

Eventually, they find a crack in our armour, a way to grab our attention, a heartstring to pull and then we're caught. No longer are we the distant observer, now we're part of the scenery.

Moving to Britain has made me keenly aware of this. I grew up in a British household in America. My English father has always taken an uncompromising attitude towards America, where he has now lived since 1969. Although I didn't move to Britain until I was almost forty, I've always felt to a degree British, if of a colonial variety. I studied British history, read British literature, enjoyed British comedies like *The Goon Show*, *Beyond the Fringe* and *Monty Python* and listened attentively to my father's stories about growing up and being a young man in England. But it was only when I moved to Britain in 2008 that I realized just how un-British I am. From almost the moment I arrived, countless unfamiliarities pressed themselves upon me (often in hilarious ways), making me feel for the first time in my life like an American. Twelve years later, I still remain a 'Yank', but my inhabiting of this excessively wet, supposedly 'sceptred isle' has enabled me now to be at home here. I know Britain in a way that not all the books, films and dreamy Anglophilia could have taught me had I continued to live in the States.

I've learned that there is knowledge that remains beyond our reach until we become vulnerable. What a strange epiphany this was! We live in an age dominated, as it has been now for more than three hundred years, by science. By its very nature, science seeks to stand apart, to take on the guise of the dispassionate observer, studying its subjects from a protected vantage where it can set aside emotional commitments in favour of reliable and repeatable facts. I've learned, however, that however useful such knowledge is, it can never achieve the kind of knowledge that comes through being a subject, a part of the scene, immersed in what one is experiencing. Knowing from within is accurate in ways that knowing from without can never be. This is why so often when others are describing the 'facts' of something we've experienced, we constantly want to interject, 'yes, but . . .' Even when the facts are presented accurately, we feel that a world of meaning has been neglected.

Inhabiting places is essential, I think, to our humanity. Taking on a scientific viewpoint is a useful tool, but if it becomes more than a tool then it starts to dehumanize us. We lose the kind of knowledge that comes from being implicated in a world in which we're inextricably involved. To be human is not only to act but to be acted upon, which is what it means to inhabit or to belong. When I study maps and read guides about the places where I'm about to go trekking, I relate to those places in a way utterly different than when I'm in them for days on end. To stand open to that world – to the goods and ills it offers – is to be human. To strive for anything different is ultimately to try to be a second-rate god. That never ends well as I suspect both our climate crisis and our fracturing sense of community and self are now teaching us.

The intensity of my inhabiting briefly the meaning-laden landscape of Cadair Idris, allowed the paradoxes I encountered to act upon me with force. I grapple with ideas like timelessness, thick time, silence and narratives all the time – I am a theologian after all. Even ideas about wonder and the ordinary aren't unfamiliar to me, as my theological research has long focused on the concept of delight, which could be defined as enjoying the wonderful in the everyday. But it was only when I inhabited the landscape of Cadair Idris on those two autumnal days that I understood those ideas from *within*. It was only then that they together acted upon me and imparted their gift of perspective. I discovered then that these paradoxes aren't something to be understood because they're infinitely beyond my grasping. They're mysteries that must be inhabited so that among them I may be at home.

I suppose I began to understand what the medieval theologians meant when they suggested that wisdom comes less from book learning than from contemplating the unsearchable mystery of God in the silence of love. If the Creator is love, then all things must be fashioned from and sustained by love. And if that's the case, then the profoundest way to understand that creation (including ourselves) is by loving it. Here again we're pushed back to the metaphor of marriage. What deeper understanding of another is available than that which arises gradually through faithful commitment 'for better, for worse'? A long-married couple enjoy a mutual comprehension they could never explain to others. In fact, that understanding through love is so powerful that they can wrap themselves in it, wordlessly sharing what no words could ever articulate.

That creation is filled utterly with the love of God is the lesson Cadair Idris impressed deeply on me. What really resolved the apparent paradoxes and juxtapositions I encountered on that Welsh mountain is love. God's love is such that not even opposites can resist being reconciled because love permits no distance, no absence, no contradiction. By allowing my heart to stand open to the book of creation, I was taught in those two days that in the deep and mysterious currents of God's love one can begin to understand what it truly means to be redeemed. In the words of Wendell Berry:

> I take literally the statement in the Gospel of John that God loves the world. I believe that the world was created and approved by love, that it subsists, coheres, and endures by love, and that, insofar as it is redeemable, it can be redeemed only by love. I believe that divine love, incarnate and indwelling in the world, summons the world always toward wholeness, which ultimately is reconciliation and atonement with God.[2]

Perhaps that's the final lesson Cadair Idris taught me. We so surround ourselves with noise, frenetic activity and clutter that we stand little chance of finding the Cwm Cau of our faith: that place where we can discover God in the depths of reality and in the deep silence of his Word who forever calls us back to our true home. We need to learn to let go, to allow ourselves to be small, inconsequential, the fleeting creatures of dust that we are. Then we might just stand a chance of discovering the vastness of Christ's Body, whose own deep history and deep stories faithfully convey the unchanging life of God. Then, in the deep silence of that encounter we may just possibly discover ourselves.

-o0o-

Alas, we find ourselves in a world that seems intent on flattening out the eternal, detaching itself from its own memory, crowding out the silence of God in the cacophony of entertainment, draining words of their meanings and evocative power and debasing what's wonderful while denigrated the merely ordinary. We seem to have chosen at some point to start walking in the opposite direction from the way that leads to wholeness and true well-being. We're like mountaineers so convinced they're on the right path that they don't stop to take their bearings even when they find themselves knee-

---

[2]Wendell Berry, 'Health Is Membership', in Norman Wirzba, *The Art of the Commonplace*, 146.

deep in a swamp. In fact, we've been in that swamp so long, we're in danger of forgetting about the mountains. And so, we continue to walk apart from the paradoxes I encountered. But like Penelope longing for her wandering husband Odysseus, creation yearns for our return, for us to find ourselves again at home with her and her Creator.

And I think we yearn for that return, too. The popularity of spirituality – as superficial as it often is – reminds us that even immersed in the banality of consumer culture, many people instinctively know that there's more to life, that below the surface of our busy lives lurks something rich and enduring. Our nihilistic choice to believe that there's no meaning, no truth, no richer layers to reality, is really no choice at all. In that direction lies only loneliness, the destruction of both the natural world and us and a crushing anxiety we can never quite shake off but only numb with regular doses of escapism. In moments of spiritual lucidity, we reach out (despite ourselves) towards God and ourselves, glimpsing ever so briefly our souls dwelling on the threshold of the divine.

'You move us to delight in praising You; for You have made us for Yourself, and our hearts are restless until they rest in You,' wrote Augustine at the start of his *Confessions*.[3] Our hearts were formed to find their rest in God amid his creation. That's our homeland, the place where we most belong. While we remain in exile, our hearts roam restlessly, unable to settle for long, always searching for rest and peace. For too many of us, to be human is to be a wanderer, moving from one relationship to another, one home to another, one job to another, one fashion to another, one obsession to another.

There are two words in Welsh that encapsulate Augustine's prayer: *hiraeth* and *tangnefedd*. *Hiraeth* refers to a deep longing for one's homeland – it's more powerful than mere homesickness because it can't be soothed. *Hiraeth* accepts that contentment will remain forever elusive unless one's exile has ended. It can be deeply melancholic, gripping the heart of the exile powerfully with a yearning to taste and feel and see and hear and smell the place he or she calls home. It's so palpable that the slightest strumming of even one of our senses summons us back, recalling our imaginations to where we most belong, and thereby stoking a deep desire. This can

---

[3]Augustine, *Confessions*, 1.1.

be debased into a form of nostalgia, a revising of our memories so that our longed-for homeland becomes a golden era or a paradise of our own imagination. But *hiraeth*, rooted though it may be in romanticism, can't ultimately be reduced to nostalgia – it's more often compared to a lover longing for her beloved whom she's unlikely to see again. If so, then I think it's also an ennobling form of love, like a lover who embraces his better angels for the sake of the beloved he's lost.

Tangnefedd, on the other hand, speaks to a deep peace that's found only in God. During a *cymun bendigaid*, the Welsh-medium Eucharist, people offer the peace to each other with the word *tangnefedd*. It seeks to express, like our 'peace of God', a peace that transcends all human comprehension – a peace that's at once secure and endless; a peace that can't be disturbed by 'trouble, sorrow, need, sickness, or any other adversity' of this 'transitory life'. The biblical word for this is Sabbath: a peaceful rest that comes not from tiredness or a need to escape but from God's own *Shabbat*:

> God's rest, quite unlike our own, is not a means of escape from the pressures and strains of the world. It couldn't be, because God's world is saturated and sustained by love, and love results in *relationship* rather than alienation, *hospitality* rather than separation. God's rest is a perfect, affirming presence in the world, a presence in which others are fully acknowledged and embraced as good and beautiful. In genuine *shabbat* there is no restlessness at all because there is no other place one could possibly want to be, no other thing one could possibly want to have. . . . To be in a Sabbath frame of heart is to be able to find a riverbank worthy of a lifetime's attention and care because one now sees in it the love of God at work.[4]

Sabbath is itself another nuptial image: the lover and the beloved dwelling in each other's delight and appreciation. To experience *tangnefedd* is to find one's heart at rest because our desires have finally found the object of their sincerest love.

I believe every human being experiences *hiraeth* to some degree. Each of us yearns for *tangnefedd*, that peace that can finally satisfy

---

[4]Wirzba, *From Nature to Creation*, 75–6.

us and in which we're at home and can be truly ourselves. This deep human yearning – perhaps the basis for all our erotic loves – can be cruel, never willing to compromise by finding satisfaction in second-best. It must have its *tangnefedd* or it will resume the journey like an exiled, weary wanderer searching for his or her homeland. And if our hearts are poorly guided by our reason, then *hiraeth* will draw us down painful cul-du-sacs and along self-destructive byways. This can happen individually with broken relationships, substance abuse, addiction and escapism, or it can happen socially with mass entertainment, affluent ease and even noble causes.

Perhaps this *hiraeth* is calling you on a pilgrimage not unlike my own up Cadair Idris. If so, then within the paradox of the eternal and the temporal, may you find purpose and meaning in the nuptial embrace of God and his creation. In the paradox of silence and words, may you find purpose and meaning in the nuptial embrace of God and your soul. Finally, in the paradox of wonder and the commonplace, may you find purpose and meaning in the nuptial union of God's glory with every atom of his creation.

The end of that pilgrimage is *tangnefedd*: a peace that surpasses anything you or I can comprehend. To discover that Sabbath rest is to discover the God who made and redeemed you, the beauty and wonder of the creation in which you belong, and your truest self. To inhabit *tangnefedd* is to dwell in the Holy of Holies, where heaven and earth cohabit and where the distance between God and his creation evaporates. Because we're sinners, that world will forever elude us in this life like an ever-vanishing horizon. Nevertheless, *hiraeth* and hearts homed by faith will reliably guide us up God's holy mountain to ever more breathtaking vistas.

Cadair Idris taught me that eternity and time, silence and words, wonder and the ordinary are the foundations of my Christian identity, manifested in the Incarnation of our sacraments, especially baptism and the Eucharist. The paradoxes show us – and how we do need to be shown! – that God's command, 'What God has joined together, let no one separate', lies at the heart of our purpose as human beings. The world in which we now live, flooded though it may be by mass entertainment, constant stimulation and easy titillation that mask an underlying fear and despair – this world yearns for a creation that's still in the palm of God's hand and utterly enchanted with God's delight.

I won't pretend that my two days on Cadair Idris marked the end of my pilgrimage of faith. I'm not sure it was even a beginning. But it was an experience that taught me unexpected, un-looked-for lessons just at a point when I needed to learn them. They also gave me something solid on which to set my feet during the storms of my middle-aged life. I went to Cadair Idris to spend two days on my own only to discover later that God was with me the whole time. I went as a recreational backpacker but returned a pilgrim. In that way, I suppose, I did have a mountaintop epiphany after all, though more in hindsight and through reflection than through some overwhelming sense of God's presence atop Penygadair. Or was it his still, small voice, speaking to my heart through the paradoxes I had found?

In any case, I'm not too worried about what further lessons I still must learn. There are many more mountains for me to climb and my muddy boots are waiting.

BIBLIOGRAPHY

Anselm, *Proslogion*, in *The Major Works*, ed. Brian Davies and G. R. Evans (Oxford: Oxford University Press, 1998).

Aquinas, Thomas, *The Summa Theologica of St. Thomas Aquinas*, Vol. 2 (New York: Benzinger Brothers, 1947).

Auden, W. H., *For the Time Being: A Christmas Oratorio*, 'Advent', III (Princeton: Princeton University Press, 2013).

Augustine, *Confessions*, trans Henry Chadwick (Oxford: Oxford University Press, 1992).

Benedict of Nursia, *Benedict, The Rule of St. Benedict in English*, ed. O. S. B. Timothy Fry, (Collegeville: The Liturgical Press, 1982).

Berry, Wendell, 'Health Is Membership', in *The Art of the Commonplace: The Agrarian Essays of Wendell Berry* (Berkeley: Counterpoint, 2002), 144–58.

Berry, Wendell, *Life Is a Miracle: An Essay Against Modern Superstition* (Berkeley: Counterpoint, 2000).

Berry, Wendell, 'People, Land, and Community', in *The Art of the Commonplace: The Agrarian Essays of Wendell Berry* (Berkeley: Counterpoint, 2002), 182–94.

Berry, Wendell, *The Art of Loading Brush: New Agrarian Writings* (Berkeley: Counterpoint, 2019).

Berry, Wendell, 'The Work of Local Culture', in *The World-Ending Fire*, ed. Paul Kingsnorth (London: Penguin, 2017), 103–18.

Berry, Wendell, 'What Passes, What Remains', in *The Art of Loading Brush: New Agrarian Writings*, ed. Wendell Berry (Berkeley: Counterpoint, 2019), 259–68.

Bonhoeffer, Dietrich, *Letters and Papers from Prison* (Minneapolis: Fortress Press, 2010).

Catholic Church, *Roman Missal*, 3rd ed. (Chicago: Liturgical Training Publications, 2011).

Chesterton, G. K., *Orthodoxy: The Romance of Faith* (New York: Image Books, 1990).

Church of England, *Book of Common Prayer and Administration of the Sacraments and Other Rites and Ceremonies of the Church According to the Use of the Church of England* (Oxford: Oxford University Press, 1925).

Church of England, *Common Worship: Pastoral Services* (London: Church House, 2000).

Church of England, *Common Worship: Services and Prayers for the Church of England* (London: Church House, 2000).

Clavier, Mark, *Rescuing the Church from Consumerism* (London: S. P. C. K., 2013).

Cronon, Bill, *Uncommon Ground: Rethinking the Human Place in Nature* (New York: W. W. Norton & Company, 1996).

De Waal, Esther, *Seeking God: The Way of St. Benedict* (Collegeville: The Liturgical Press, 1984).

Descartes, René, *Passions of the Soul*, ar. 76, trans. Stephen Voss (Indianapolis: Hackett Publishing Co., 1989).

Doran, Michael, ed., *Conversations with Paul Cézanne* (Berkley: UC Press, 2001).

Fermor, Patrick Leigh, *A Time to Keep Silence* (London: John Murray, 1957).

Fry, Plantagenet Somerset, *Castles of the British Isles* (New York: Dorset Press, 1990).

Hempton, Gordon and John Grossmann, *One Square Inch of Silence: One Man's Quest for Silence* (New York: Free Press, 2009).

Howells, W., *Cambrian Superstitions, Comprising Ghosts, Omens, Witchcraft, Traditions, &c*, (London: Longman & Co., 1831).

Ignatius of Antioch, 'Letter to the Ephesians', in *Early Christian Writings: The Apostolic Fathers*, trans. Maxwell Staniforth (London: Penguin Books, 1968), 57–68.

Ignatius of Antioch, 'Letter to the Magnesians', in *Early Christian Writings: The Apostolic Fathers*, trans. Maxwell Staniforth (London: Penguin Books, 1968), 69–75.

John of the Cross, *Spiritual Canticle*, 'Stanza III', in *John of the Cross: Selected Writings*, ed. O. C. D. Kevin Kavanaugh (New York: Paulist Press, 1987).

John of the Cross, *The Ascent of Mount Carmel*, in *John of the Cross: Selected Writings*, ed. O. C. D. Kevin Kavanaugh (New York: Paulist Press, 1987).

Kendall, Richard, *Cézanne by Himself* (London: Time Warner Books, 2004).

Laird, Martin, *Into the Silent Land: A Guide to the Christian Practice of Contemplation* (New York: Oxford University Press, 2006).

Lewis, C. S., *Surprised by Joy: The Shape of My Early Years* (San Diego: Harcourt Brace & Company, 1955).

Lowenthal, David, *The Heritage Crusade and the Spoils of History* (Cambridge: Cambridge University Press, 1997).

MacCulloch, Diarmaid, *Silence: A Christian History* (London: Penguin, 2014).

Macfarlane, Robert, *Mountains of the Mind* (London: Granta Books, 2003).

Merton, Thomas, *The Silent Life* (New York: Farrar, Straus & Giroux, 1957).

Moltmann, Jürgen, *Crucified God: The Cross of Christ as the Foundation and Criticism of Christian Theology* (London: SCM Press, 1974).

Moor, Robert, *On Trails: An Exploration* (London: Autumn Press, 2016).

Newman, John Henry, *An Essay on the Development of Christian Doctrine* (London: James Toovey, 1845).

O'Donovan, Oliver, *Common Objects of Love, Moral Reflection and the Shaping of Community: The 2001 Stob Lectures* (Grand Rapids: William B. Eerdmans Pub., 2002).

Orr, David, *Earth in Mind: On Education, Environment, and the Human Prospect* (Washington, DC: Island Press, 2004).

Plotinus, *Enneads*, trans. Stephen MacKenna (London: Penguin, 1991).

Rebanks, James, *The Shepherd's Life: A Tale of the Lake District* (London: Penguin, 2015).

Rhind, Peter and Margaret Jones, 'The Vegetation History of Snowdonia since the Late Glacial Period', *Field Studies* 10 (2003): 539–52.

Rorty, Richard, 'Freud and Moral Reflection', *Essays on Heidegger and Others: Philosophical Papers* (Cambridge: Cambridge University Press, 1991).

Sacks, Oliver, 'My Periodic Table', *New York Times*, 24 July 2015.

Schmemann, Alexander, *For the Life of the World* (Crestwood: St Vladimir's Press, 1998).

Shusterman, Richard, 'Postmodern Aestheticism: A New Moral Philosophy?', *Theory, Culture and Society*, 5 (1988): 337–55.

Scruton, Roger, *Green Philosophy: How to Think Seriously About the Planet* (London: Atlantic Books, 2012).

'Statutes of Carthusian Monks', https://www.chartreux.org/en/carthusian-way.php, accessed 27 November 2020.

Thomas, R. S., 'AD', *Counterpoint* (Hexham: Bloodaxe Books Ltd, 1990).

Tolkien, J. R. R., *Tolkien On Fairy-stories, Expanded Edition, with Commentary and Notes*, ed. Verlyn Flieger and Douglas A. Anderson (London: HarperCollins Pub., 2008).

Traherne, Thomas, *Centuries* (New York: Harper & Brothers, 1960).

Walker, Caroline Bynum, 'Wonder', *The American Historical Review*, 102:1 (February 1997).

Walsh, James S. J., ed., *The Assessment of Inner Stirrings* in *The Pursuit of Wisdom and Other Works, by the Author of The Cloud of Unknowing* (New York: Paulist Press, 1988).

William of St-Thierry, *On Contemplating God*, VIII, in *On Contemplating God, Prayer, Meditations* trans. C. S. M. V. Penelope Lawson (Kalamazoo: Cistercian Press, 1970).

Wirzba, Norman, *From Nature to Creation: A Christian Vision for Understanding and Loving Our World* (Grand Rapids: Baker, 2015).

Wirzba, Norman, *Living the Sabbath: Discovering the Rhythms of Rest and Delight* (Grand Rapids: Brazos Press, 2006).

Wirzba, Norman, *The Art of the Commonplace: The Agrarian Essays of Wendell Berry* (Berkeley: Counterpoint, 2002).

Wolfe, Linnie M., *John of the Mountains: The Unpublished Journals of John Muir* (Madison: University of Wisconsin Press, 2009).

INDEX

Aberystwyth   10
Adam and Eve   29, 117, 138,
    163–4
aesthetics   56, 117, 127, 135–7
Alps, the   5, 68–70, 115, 142,
    152, 158
Anglicanism   xv, 3, 9, 10, 32, 160
Anglo-Saxons   50, 88, 142
Annwn   82
Anselm, Saint   26, 69
Anthropocene. *See* ecological crisis
Appalachian Mountains   xiii,
    xvii, 5, 21, 46–7, 96, 115,
    124, 146
Aquinas, Thomas   26, 140–1, 156
Ark of the Covenant   4, 8, 58, 60
art, artists   6, 51, 77, 134, 141–3,
    145, 150–4
Augustine of Hippo   28–9, 93,
    107, 108, 149, 155, 169
Avignon   5, 132

baptism   2, 32, 34, 74, 103–5,
    108–9
Barmouth   115, 129
beauty   xv, 5–6, 8, 19, 21,
    25–9, 54, 65–7, 124, 126–7,
    145–52, 159, 163–4, 171
belonging   35, 36, 44, 50, 54, 70,
    73, 88–9, 142–3, 165–7,
    169–71. *See also* inhabiting
Benedicite   9
Benedict, Saint   11, 142–3
Beowulf   85, 86

Berry, Wendell   37, 42–3, 99,
    102–3, 105, 153, 168
Bible   4, 23, 29, 30, 32–3, 60, 74,
    83–4, 87, 89, 91–2, 109,
    117, 162–4, 170
Bible Society   32–3
Bierce, Ambrose   39
Bonhoeffer, Dietrich   23
Book of Common Prayer   xv, 3
Brecon Beacons   xiii, 5, 7–8, 20,
    47–8, 80, 91, 96, 120
Brecon Cathedral   xiii, 1, 6, 71,
    87, 97, 103–4, 124
Bronze Age   34, 48, 50
Bynum, Caroline Walker   119

Cadair Idris   x, xii–xiv, 10–13,
    17–2, 35, 40, 57, 63–5,
    81–4, 86–7, 94, 113–5,
    125, 129–30, 144, 147–8,
    154, 158–62, 165, 167–8,
    171–2
Cadfan, Saint   83, 86, 87
Calvinistic Methodism   32
Cardiff   xii, 36, 49–50, 68, 87–8,
    144
Carreg yr Enwau   x, 35
Cash, Johnny   139
Castell-y-Bere   x, 33–5, 43–4
Catholicism   xiv, xv, 1–5, 8, 10,
    26, 92
Celts   44, 49, 50, 79, 88, 89, 103,
    115
Cézanne, Paul   150–2

changelessness   12, 13, 19–27,
    30, 31, 46–7, 49–50, 56–7,
    59–60, 65, 85, 86, 104, 109,
    161, 162, 167
Charles, Thomas   32
Cherokee   47, 96
Chesterton, G. K.   119–20, 148
childhood   34, 117–8
Christ, Jesus   2, 3, 23, 28, 30, 34,
    38, 59–60, 74, 90, 104–8,
    138–40, 154, 156–7, 161,
    164–5
church   1, 2, 60, 90–2, 105, 139,
    164
    of England   xii, 44, 90
    in Wales   xii, 31
churches
    interior   1–2, 92
    mega   3–4
    parish   34, 38–40, 43–4, 56,
        83
climate change. See ecological
    crisis
Cloud of Unknowing   76
commonplace   13, 39, 131–43,
    148–54, 156–7, 161,
    171
communication   3, 75–6, 78,
    92–3, 95–6, 104, 108, 151,
    152
community   34–5, 40–3, 48–50,
    53–6, 70–1, 88–9, 92, 96,
    102–3, 105, 122, 136,
    142–3, 167
conservationists   56, 66, 123
consumerism   44, 52, 55, 84–5,
    89, 100, 131, 133, 136,
    145–6, 168–9, 171. See also
    globalism
contemplation   11, 19, 58–9,
    65–7, 78, 131, 146, 157,
    164, 167
cosmos   26, 65, 68, 107
Cotswolds   xvii, 27, 32, 47

Covid-19   xiv, 71, 126
craftsmanship   145
Craig Lwyd   14, 63–4, 71, 113
Craig yr Aderyn   34
Cranmer, Thomas   3
creation   2–5, 8–10, 23–4, 26,
    28–30, 52, 72, 78, 93,
    104–7, 109, 117, 122–4,
    147, 149, 151–2, 154–7,
    161–5, 167–9, 171
    new   164
Cronon, Bill   52–3
crucifixion   58, 91, 107
Crug Hywel   49
culture   57, 85, 86, 102–3, 135
Cwm Cau   x, 12, 14, 15, 17–7,
    30, 46, 57, 64, 65, 81–2, 94,
    113–4, 168

dead, the   xiv, 2, 30–3, 40, 41,
    45, 81, 90, 96–101, 103,
    137–8
death   22, 29, 34, 43, 48, 56,
    58, 59, 65–6, 97, 99–101,
    137–9
delight   xvii, 6, 8, 12–13, 19, 25,
    26, 69, 72, 118–21, 126–7,
    141, 148–50, 152–4, 161,
    163–5, 167, 169–71
Descartes, René   121–2
desire   8, 28, 52–3, 76–7, 122,
    124–6, 134, 135, 140–2,
    161, 169–70
devil   74, 83
De Waal, Esther   142–3
disenchantment   120–4
Disney   56, 84
dogs (Cuthbert and Humphrey)
    xvii, 5–7, 49–50, 72, 80, 82,
    94, 97, 113, 124, 130
Dolwyddelan   49
dualism   161–4
Dysynni Valley   xvi, 31–47, 57,
    63, 83, 114, 130, 144

East Anglia 32
Easter 2–4, 38, 59
ecological crisis 29–30, 41, 70–1,
    122, 136–7, 153, 167
Eden 4, 30, 91, 117, 159, 163–4
Edward I 33–4, 44
Elijah 11, 29, 73, 74
escapism 41, 70, 73, 133, 169,
    171
eternity 12, 18–19, 23–7, 57–60,
    63, 65–6, 101, 103, 106,
    109, 143, 171. *See also*
    timelessness
Eucharist 2–3
Exodus 23, 58, 91
Exsultet 3–4
Ezekiel 105–6

fairies 6, 80–3, 86, 93, 120, 122,
    123
faith xiv, xvi, 10, 13, 36, 51, 53,
    56, 89, 93, 104, 105, 107–9,
    125, 139–40, 160–5, 167–8,
    171–2
familiarity 7, 35–7, 66, 119–20,
    124
Fan Fawr 7–8, 27
farmers, farming 7, 18, 31, 33,
    35, 37–9, 55, 57, 93, 95, 96,
    102–3, 130, 153
Fermor, Patrick Leigh 131
Fforest Fawr 47–8
fields 5, 7, 20, 31, 33, 37–8, 47,
    49, 56, 121, 132
folktales 79–87, 94, 122
Francis, Saint 5
Fry, Plantagenet Somerset 33
funerals 31–2, 49, 97–9, 137–8

gardeners, gardening 29–30,
    153–4
Genesis 89, 93, 104, 107, 162–4
geology 12, 18, 20, 21, 29, 87,
    147

globalism 40–1, 84–5, 124–5,
    146
glory 4, 8, 11, 49, 58, 60, 105–6,
    112, 136, 138, 140, 149,
    154, 156, 171
Glyder Fach 20, 27
goodness 62, 149, 159, 163–4
Graig Goch 63
Greeks 58, 59, 85–6, 88, 108,
    164
Grenoble 5, 132
Gwyn ap Nudd 82, 85, 87, 93,
    113

heaven 1–3, 4, 8–9, 19, 28, 30,
    57–60, 62, 78, 91–3, 104–6,
    109, 112, 149, 156–7,
    161–5, 171
Hempton, Gordon 70–1
Henry III 33
Herbert, George 157
heritage xiii, xiv, 37–9, 42, 51–5,
    84, 158
hill forts 44, 48–9, 56, 79–80, 96
hiraeth 13–14, 169–71
history 12, 21, 32, 34, 40, 44,
    46, 48–9, 51, 57, 60, 81, 97,
    143, 158, 165–6, 168
    thick (*see* thick time)
Holy Spirit 2–3, 58, 78
home xiv, 13–14, 27, 30, 35–9,
    41–2, 45, 49, 54–5, 57,
    72–3, 86, 88–9, 101–2, 109,
    129, 142–3, 165–71
Hopkins, Gerard Manley 8
humility 44, 117, 123–4, 126,
    127, 139–42, 153
husbandry 152

Iceland xvii, 5, 80, 115, 144
identity 41, 44–5, 60, 89, 171
Idris the Giant 17, 81–3, 86, 87,
    113, 115
Ignatius of Antioch, Saint 106–7

imagination　14, 24, 27, 35, 36,
　39, 44, 45, 60, 79–80, 84–6,
　91–4, 96, 106, 118, 119,
　126, 144, 150–2, 169–70
immutability. *See* changelessness
industry　43, 46, 50–6, 146
inhabiting　36, 44, 59, 73,
　143, 165–8, 171. *See also*
　belonging
internet　145–6
Iron Age　34, 50
Israel　58, 60, 74, 90, 139

John of the Cross, Saint　11, 108
Jones, Mary　32–5, 65, 83, 86,
　87, 129
joy　xvii, 10, 73, 78, 104, 118–9,
　122, 125–6, 149

Kalevala　81
King Arthur　82, 87, 122
Kingdom of God　28, 90, 139,
　157

Laird, Martin　69, 108
Lake District　xvii, 54–6, 123
landscapes　xiii–xiv, 2, 5–8, 12–3,
　19–22, 24–7, 42–3, 55, 65,
　67–8, 73, 88, 94–5, 121,
　131, 133, 147, 159, 165–6
　historical　34–5, 37–8, 44–51,
　　53–4, 56–7, 79–87, 96, 101,
　　159, 167
　sacred　84, 88–9, 91–3
Lang, Andrew　123
legends　12, 79–84, 86–8, 91, 94
Lewis, C. S.　5, 125–6
light　3–8, 64–5, 107, 118, 127,
　145, 162–3
limits　53, 89, 128, 140, 143
liturgy　xv, 1, 3–4, 90–3
Livy　81
Llandaff Cathedral　7

Llanfihangel-y-pennant　14,
　31–5, 37, 83, 103, 160
Llyn Bochlwyd　20
Llyn Cau　xi, 12, 13, 17–8, 31,
　34, 61, 87, 94, 113, 114
Llyn y Gadair　20, 129
Llywelyn Fawr　33
Logos (the Word)　74–5, 90, 93,
　104–5, 107–8
longing　xiv, 13, 85, 125–6, 155.
　See also hiraeth
love　xiii, xiv, 3, 5, 8, 11, 13,
　24–6, 28, 36, 39–40, 42–3,
　56, 66, 71, 73, 76–8, 80–1,
　84, 93, 95, 102, 104–5,
　108–9, 124–6, 137–8, 157,
　160–8, 170–1
Lowenthal, David　51
Loxahatchee River　27

Mabinogion　81
Macfarlane, Robert　116
Macsen Wledig　48
Maen Llia　48
management　51–5, 57, 120–1
Marcher Lords　33, 50
marriage　xiii, 17–18, 49, 56,
　132, 144, 155, 157, 160,
　162–5, 167
media, mass　35, 41, 84, 85, 102,
　130, 133–6, 145–6, 152
memory　34–5, 37, 40, 42–3, 48,
　54, 96, 98–100, 102, 118,
　168
Merton, Thomas　72–3
Minffordd Path　17, 113
modernity　10, 35–6, 50, 52,
　64, 70–1, 77, 101–3, 116,
　121–2, 127, 130, 131,
　133–4, 138, 143, 145, 155
Moltmann, Jürgen　24
monastery　4, 11, 50, 83, 87, 131,
　142–3

monasticism 74–5, 131, 142–3
monuments 38–9, 44, 49–51,
    145
Moor, Robert 21
moors 20, 47–8
Morgan ap Rhys 82–3, 86
Moses 11, 23, 29, 74, 112
mountains xi, xiii, 5, 9, 11–13,
    21–2, 32, 34, 46–9, 57,
    63–5, 68, 73–4, 87, 96,
    112, 114–6, 123, 129–30,
    132
Muir, John 66, 123
Munch, Edvard 77
music 4, 5, 68, 71–2, 152
mystery 26–7, 29, 78, 122,
    150–1, 162, 167
myths 12, 79, 81–2, 84–9, 91,
    92, 138

names x–xi, xvi, 13, 35, 83, 95,
    97, 104
field 37
place 46–9, 80, 87–8, 91
Narnia 80, 125, 127
national parks 10, 70, 96, 123
nature xiii, xiv, 2–3, 5–10, 13,
    25–30, 46–7, 52–4, 56,
    64, 66, 68–71, 80, 90, 94,
    96, 107, 118–9, 123, 124,
    145–7, 150–1, 153–4, 159,
    160
Neoplatonism 25, 68–70, 74,
    159
Newman, John Henry 22
Njal's Saga 80
noise 12, 18, 64, 65, 67, 68,
    70–3, 76, 104, 107, 131,
    168
Norse 79, 80
Norway 5, 68–70, 158
nostalgia 39, 42, 43, 56, 85, 170.
    See also hiraeth

nuptial union 59, 161, 163–5,
    170, 171

ordinariness. See commonplace
Orr, David 118, 126–7
Oxford xiii, xiv, 5, 7, 36, 132,
    144, 160
Oxfordshire xii, xvii, 6–7, 38–9,
    47, 99

parables 28, 95, 136, 139, 154,
    164
paradox 8–10, 12–14, 26–7, 46,
    57–60, 92, 101–3, 106–9,
    157, 161–5, 171
peace 13–14, 66, 72–3, 76, 78,
    162–3. See also tangnefedd
Pen y Crug 49, 96
Penygadair xi, 10, 14, 17, 111,
    113–5, 123–4, 129, 144,
    172
Physicians of Myddfai 81
pilgrimage xiv, xvii, 13–4, 48,
    84, 159, 160, 162, 171–2
Pisgah National Forest 91, 96,
    146
Plato 22, 59
Plotinus 57, 68–9
poetry 12, 77, 81, 82, 84, 87, 91,
    93, 94, 106, 157
Potter, Beatrix 55
preaching 4, 83, 90, 105–6, 109
Pride and Prejudice 22
Pyrenees 5, 158

rationalism 26–7, 92, 120, 121,
    125, 127
Rebanks, James 54–5
Resurrection 2–4, 30, 59, 90,
    91, 139
reverence 19, 50–2, 122, 123,
    149
Rhiw Gwredydd 129–30

Romans   xii, 3, 34–5, 44, 48–50, 88–91, 139, 145
Rorty, Richard   135

Sabbath   72, 170–1
Sacks, Oliver   65–6
sacraments   xv, 2–5, 8, 10, 34, 104–5, 156, 171. *See also* baptism; Eucharist
St Michael's College   xii, 7, 17–18, 31, 132, 160
saints   1, 11–12, 39, 60, 83, 87, 115, 135, 139–40
Sarn Helen   48
Schmemann, Alexander   156–7
science   29, 43, 121, 161, 166
Scruton, Roger   41–2
seasons   2, 6–7, 20–1, 35, 46, 91–2
self, inner   25–6, 28, 45, 60, 66–7, 72–3, 75–8, 96, 117, 119, 135, 140, 167, 171
senses   1, 5–6, 19, 20, 132, 150–2, 169
sentimentalism   39–40, 42
Shakespeare, William   85, 164
shepherds   29, 35, 54–5, 83
Shining Rock Wilderness   27, 47, 124
Shusterman, Richard   135
silence   12, 13, 61, 63–78, 81, 93–8, 100–9, 131, 143, 146, 157, 161, 162, 165, 167–8, 171
Snowdonia   5, 10, 17, 32, 63, 158
solitude   5–6, 19, 66–70, 72–5, 77, 161, 163
sound. *See* noise
spirituality   142, 169
stability   35, 36, 53, 138, 142–3
standing stones   34, 44, 47–8

stories   12, 35–6, 39–40, 46, 53–4, 77–9, 95–9, 107–9, 118, 123, 165, 168
sublimity   12–13, 25
Sunnmøre Alps. *See* Norway
symbols   1, 3–4, 92, 105–6, 157, 164

tangnefedd   xi, 14, 169–71
Tertullian   18
theophany   11–2, 172
Thomas, R. S.   77
time   2, 7, 12, 13, 18–19, 21–4, 26, 34, 38, 41–2, 44–7, 57–61, 63, 67–9, 85, 86, 99–101, 103, 105–6, 131, 161, 162, 171. *See also* history; thick
thick   32–40, 42–54, 56–7, 60, 65, 81, 84–6, 102–5, 109, 161, 167
timelessness. *See* changelessness
Tolkien, J. R. R.   5, 120
Traherne, Thomas   67, 112, 148–9, 153
treks   xvii, 8, 10, 20, 30, 34, 68, 83, 130–2, 141, 148, 158, 167
tribalism   40–1
Twyn y Gaer   xi, 49

Virgil   81
Virgin Mary   26, 58, 60, 107

Wales   xii–xiv, 5–7, 10, 17, 22, 33, 34, 36, 37, 46–51, 81–3, 87–8, 91, 96, 114, 132, 144, 148, 149, 158, 160
walking   xiii, xiv, xvi–xvii, 5–8, 13, 19, 21, 32, 36, 37, 46–8, 55, 57, 59, 66–8, 72, 79–80, 97, 124–5, 132, 146–7, 158–60, 165

Weber, Max   120
wilderness   14, 18, 20, 21, 24–5,
   27, 29, 30, 47, 52–4, 57, 64,
   68, 74, 91, 124, 130–1, 144,
   146, 151
William of St-Thierry   78, 104
Wirzba, Norman   72, 141–2,
   150–1, 163–4, 170
wonder   2, 5, 12–3, 18, 25, 29,
   52, 87, 115–30, 132–6,
   138, 140, 145–9, 151–8,

161–3, 165, 167, 168,
   171
   sense of   117–23, 127–8, 148
words   12–13, 75–8, 81, 83–4,
   87–93, 93–6, 105–9, 143,
   157, 161, 162, 167, 168,
   171
worship   xv, 1–2, 4–5, 8–10, 12,
   30, 48, 56, 60, 89–92, 127

Yosemite   54, 123